FLY GIRL

BY GENEVIEVE HEGNEY & CATHERINE MOORE

CURRENCY PRESS
The performing arts publisher

CURRENT THEATRE SERIES

First published in 2025
by Currency Press Pty Ltd,
Gadigal Land, Suite 310, 46–56 Kippax Street, Surry Hills, NSW 2010, Australia
enquiries@currency.com.au
www.currency.com.au

in association with Ensemble Theatre

Typeset by Brighton Gray for Currency Press.
Printed by Fineline Print + Copy Services, Revesby, NSW.
Cover shows Catherine Moore and Genevieve Hegney; photo by Brett Boardman.
Cover design by Alphabet Studio.

Currency Press acknowledges the Traditional Owners of the Country on which we live and work. We pay our respects to all Aboriginal and Torres Strait Islander Elders, past and present.

A catalogue record for this
book is available from the
National Library of Australia

Contents

Fly Girl was first produced by Ensemble Theatre, Cammeraygal Country, Kirribilli, on 17 October 2025 with the following cast and creatives:

DEBORAH LAWRIE (DEB)	Cleo Meinck
PETER WARDLEY, HELEN, GARTH, BRUCE, CAPTAIN TOMLIN & VARIOUS	Alex Kirwan
MUM, MARGARET, RICHARD, CAPTAIN BURNETT, DWYER & VARIOUS	Emma Palmer
PATRICIA, PAMELA, REG, TODD, HENRY, TRISH & VARIOUS	Genevieve Hegney
GLENDA, FAY, KENNETH, FRANK, CAPTAIN BALL, MARY & VARIOUS	Catherine Moore

Director, Janine Watson
Set and Costume Designer, Grace Deacon
Lighting Designer, Morgan Moroney
Composer and Sound Designer, Daniel Herten
Stage Manager, Zoe Davis
Assistant Stage Manager, Alexis Worthing
Costume Supervisor, Renata Beslik

CHARACTERS

AIR TRAFFIC CONTROLLER
ANGRY HAYDEN
ANSETT LAWYERS
BOSS V/O
BRADLEY
BRUCE
CAPTAIN BALL
CAPTAIN BRUCE V/O
CAPTAIN BURNETT
CAPTAIN HENRY THEUNISSEN
CAPTAIN SPENCER V/O
CAPTAIN TOMLIN
CAROL REINER
CAROLYN KINGHAM
DAD
DEBORAH LAWRIE
DEIDRE FITZGERALD
DON RYAN
JOHN DWYER
FAY MARLES
FIRST OFFICER BRUCE WOODBRIDGE
FRANK PASCOE
GARTH
GIRL
GLENDA
GRAEME
HELEN
HOSTESS ANNOUNCEMENT
IAN SHARP
JANA WENDT
KENNETH
MARGARET
MARY
MR ARTHUR
MR KING
MR TYLER MOORE
MR WHITE
MUM
PAMELA GRAHAM
PATRICIA
PETER
PILOT
RACE CALLER V/O
RADIO ANNOUNCEMENT V/O
REG ANSETT
REG'S WIFE
REPORTERS
RICHARD
RYAN
SCHUMANN
SHARP
STUDENT
TED
TODD
TREVER
TRISH
YOUNG WOMAN

This playtext went to press before the end of rehearsals and may differ from the play as performed.

SETTING

Melbourne, Australia, 1965–1980.

STYLE NOTES

/ indicates that the remainder of the speech is spoken simultaneously with the dialogue that follows.

PROLOGUE

CROSSING THE LINE. RACE TRACK. 1965.

A twelve-year-old DEBORAH LAWRIE [DEB]*; tall for her age, confident but not showy, and bright as a button, stands at the Flemington Racecourse with her* DAD *as the final stage of a race is called.*

RACE CALLER: [*voiceover*] … and it's *Chariots Chance* out in front by half a length but coming up on the outside is *Legs To Heaven …*

DAD: Come on.

DEB: Gooooo Legs To Heaven!

RACE CALLER: [*voiceover*] *Legs To Heaven* takes the lead as she strides away from the pack and she's gonna bring it home; it's *Legs To Heaven* by a nose, followed by *Chariots Chance* and half a head away, *Virgin Bride* comes in third.

The RACE CALLER *fades out as* DAD *and* DEB *step forward.*

DAD: You bewdy.

DEB: We won! We won!!!

DAD: Beginner's luck.

DEB: Daaaad.

DAD: You keep backing winners, Deb, you'll fast become my favourite.

DEB: I'm already your favourite.

DEB *smiles. She knows she is.*

DAD: I'm gonna grab a beer. You want a lemon squash?

DEB: I'll come.

DAD: Uh-uh. Men only.

DEB: What d'ya mean?

DAD *motions to A LINE ON THE GROUND in front of him.*

DAD: Ladies aren't allowed to cross this line.

DEB: I'm only twelve, Dad.

DAD: Girls aren't either.

DEB: Why not?

DAD: It's the rules.

DAD *moves off.*

DEB: What happens if they do?
DAD: You're not gonna be the one to find out. Want a squash or not?
DEB: If I'm *allowed.*

DAD *smiles and heads off.*

DAD: Wait here.

The first strains of Norman Greenbaum's 'Spirit in the Sky' start up.

DEB *stares at the line in front of her. How far it runs in both directions. She looks round to make sure she's not being watched ... The lights fade till there's just a spotlight on* DEB. *Slowly,* DEB *slides her foot to touch the line.* DEB *looks down at her foot again. Will she slide it over? She takes a breath, looks at her foot once more ...*

Blackout.

FLYING LESSONS. MOORABBIN AIRPORT. CAR PARK. 1969.

The sounds of Moorabbin Airport. DEB, *sixteen, and her* DAD *pull up in a car. 'Spirit in the Sky' still plays on the radio. Happy together in their own worlds. They wind down their windows and take a collective whiff of the air. The song fades out.*

DAD: Kerosene.
DEB: Burnt rubber.
DAD: Freedom.

Beat. DEB *leans forward and pulls a Flight Manual out of the glovebox.*

DEB: You've got five minutes before your lesson, Dad. I'll test you.

She opens the book and inside is an envelope that reads DEB. *She holds it up.*

What's this?
DAD: Heard it's someone's birthday coming up. Happy Sweet Sixteen, Deb.

DEB *unfolds excitedly, reads.*

DEB: [*a little bemused*] Flying lessons?

DAD: You like coming up with me and Garth.

DEB: Yeah … I just didn't expect it.

DAD: I'll take them back / if that's your attitude.

DEB: No, no, no, no Dad. I wanna give it a go!

DEB *starts to warm to the idea.*

Thanks, Dad.

DAD: Just the two. After that you pay for yourself.

DEB: Course. Do you reckon I'll be any good?

DAD: You're already ahead of me on theory.

DAD *motions to the Flight Manual.*

Go on.

DEB: *What is the 'order of priorities' when flying?*

DAD: Aviate, Navigate, Communicate.

DEB: Correct. *What are the four forces that act on an aircraft?*

DAD: Lift, Weight, Thrust and Drag?

DEB: *What does carby heat do?*

DAD: Umm … something to do with using hot air to … Pass.

Without looking, DEB *rattles the answer off.*

DEB: Prevents build up of ice in the carburetor. Come on Dad, you should know that.

DAD: We can't all be as smart as you, Deb.

DEB: Actually Mr Thompson gave us some really tricky homework I need your help with … you home tonight?

DAD: I'm off to the races.

DEB: … Can I come?

DAD: Not this time.

DEB: Haven't let me for ages.

DAD *doesn't respond.*

Can you help tomorrow morning, then?

DAD: It'll be a late one. I'll be staying with someone who lives near the track.

DEB: Who?

Beat.

DAD: Gimme another one.

DEB: *What is the secondary effect of aileron?*

DAD: Oh I never remember this. Ahhhh.

DEB: Bzzzz.

DEB *makes a fishtail motion with her hand.*

Yaw!

DAD: Well, two out of four ain't bad.

DEB: Two out of four ain't good either. If you don't pass the theory, you won't be able to fly solo.

DAD: Well, that's not an option.

DEB: Why are you so obsessed with flying solo, Dad?

DAD: It's the pinnacle, Deb. They say there's no better feeling. When you're up there on your own, you find out what you're made of.

Beat. DAD *sees his instructor,* GARTH, *arriving.*

There's Garth. You coming up?

DEB: Nah, I'll just wait down here, do my homework.

DAD: Right you are.

DAD *heads off and* DEB *watches him go. She reaches for her homework, looks at it for a moment, throws it down and picks up the Flight Manual instead. She opens it and starts to read.*

PERSISTENCE. REG INTERVIEW. REG'S HOME OFFICE. 1969.

An interview between REG ANSETT*—sixty, quiet confidence and a never-say-die attitude hidden behind a smile—and a* REPORTER.

REPORTER: Tonight we have a very special guest, Sir Reginald Ansett, newly knighted for his Service to Aviation. Firstly, may I say congratulations, Sir.

REG: It's a … yes, it's a real honour.

REPORTER: Sir Reginald, I understand your beginnings weren't in aviation but road transport?

REG: That's right. I had ten quid in my pocket and put a deposit on a second-hand Studebaker and started a one-man car service operation between Ballarat and Maryborough.

REPORTER: And within a few short years, you had built up a fleet of cars?

REG: That's right.

REPORTER: Isn't it true you were so successful that Robert Menzies, Victorian Transport Minister at the time, pushed a bill through State parliament *prohibiting* service cars from *competing* with Victorian Rail?

REG: That's right.

REPORTER: And it was that, in turn, that forced you to turn your hand to air service?

REG: Well, the skies were controlled by the *Commonwealth* Government, so the *State* government couldn't ... couldn't stand in our way.

REPORTER: And now you run Australia's biggest airline. I've spoken with a number of your colleagues who've described you as down-to-earth, unpretentious, a man with a vision. But almost all say you have a great deal of persistence. Would you say that's accurate?

REG: I would. I don't think I'm anything out of the box. I just think if you ahhh, work hard enough and long enough, you'll get somewhere.

REPORTER: Sir Reginald, you have a framed quote next to your desk. May I ask you to share it?

REG: Certainly. '*Nothing can take the place of persistence ...* '

Overlap interview.

YOU'LL MARRY A PLANE. DEB'S FAMILY LOUNGE ROOM. 1969.

Lights fade up on DEB, *who sits in an armchair in a modest family living room. She imagines she's in the cockpit of a small aircraft.* DEB *mimes the actions as she goes through her checklist.*

DEB: [*mouthing*] Pre-flight checks. Park Break set. Trim set. Master on. Mixture rich. Primer locked. Flaps set. Fuel on fullest tank. Fuel pump on. Instruments Check. Ignition Check. Power up. Left. Right. Both. Controls full and free. Harnesses and hatches secure. Cleared for take off.

REG: ' ... *Talent will not; nothing is more common than unsuccessful men with talent. Genius will not; unrewarded genius is almost a proverb. Education will not; the world is full of educated derelicts. Persistence and determination alone are omnipotent.'*

Lights out on REG *and* REPORTER.

MUM: [*off*] Debbie. Come set the table.

DEB: Check clear of other aircraft.

MUM: [*off*] Debbie?! Come set the damn table!

DEB: Line up.

MUM: Deborah Jane Lawrie!!

MUM *strides into the room.*

DEB: Shit, Mum.

MUM: Don't speak like that, it's not ladylike.

DEB: You said 'damn'.

MUM: That's different, it's tradition.

Beat.

Why are you wearing pants? You're not Katherine Hepburn.

DEB: I just had a lesson, Mum. I can't fly in a skirt, can I?

MUM: Why not?

DEB: Don't you notice *anything*? I always wear jeans / when I fly!!

MUM: I'm a little distracted by a job, a house and four kids to take note of your outfits—

DEB: You never listen / to me.

MUM: That's not / true.

DEB: I told you. At my very first lesson, I get in the plane and Garth asks me to adjust the seat, remember?

MUM: It's ringing / a bell.

DEB: So I put my hand under the seat and I'm feelin' around like a blind man in the dark and he says '*You know, it works like a car seat*?' And I say '*But I can't drive yet, Garth.*' He tries to explain about a hundred times, and I keep trying and trying but I can't work the bloody / thing out.

MUM: Language, Debbie!

DEB: So out of desperation he leans over, grabs the lever under the seat and wham, yanks the seat forward. I pushed my skirt down, real quick, so he didn't feel uncomfortable but it was *so* embarrassing. I felt like such a dork, Mum! So, I wear pants when I fly now.

MUM: Come set the table!

MUM *exits.*

DEB: I have to practise my checklists!!

MUM [*off*]: Chores first. Hobbies later.

DEB: It's not a hobby / Mum!

MUM *re-enters.*

MUM: I thought you weren't that fussed about flying. Now you spend every weekend mowing lawns, washing cars, delivering papers to pay for the lessons. Lessons to which I have to drive you and wait in the car like / some kind of chauffeur.

DEB: It's only once a month / Mum!

MUM: And every spare minute at home you're turning my lounge into a cockpit.

DEB: Well, I have to keep practising because if I don't I'll never fly solo and if I don't fly solo, what's the point of / any of this?

MUM: Why's it so important to fly solo?

DEB: Dad says—

MUM: Your dad says a lot of things.

DEB: Well, he understands me!

MUM: I'm sure he / does.

DEB: We speak the same language!

MUM: That might be so but he's not here anymore, is he?!

DEB: Coz that bitch / has her claws in him!

MUM: Language / Debbie!

DEB: And she's told Dad he can't / see us!

MUM: Your father's a grown man. He makes his own decisions.

DEB: But you could fight, Mum?! You're such a bloody victim!

MUM: He's not here coz he doesn't want to be. And nothing I say is going to change that!

DEB *is quietened by this. Beat. Begrudgingly, she gets out of the armchair and heads out to set the table.*

It's just not natural for a girl to be so obsessed.

DEB: I'll set the table, Mum. What more do you want?!

MUM: I want you to be like other girls, Debbie. Find a nice boy, hang out with your friends, have some fun.

DEB: I have to finish what I've started!

Beat.

MUM: Five more minutes. Then come set the table.
DEB: Thanks, Mum.

DEB *jumps back in the chair.* MUM *turns to leave, then turns back.*

MUM: But you better watch out Debbie, you'll marry a plane at this rate.

MUM *leaves.* DEB *settles back into her makeshift cockpit.*

DEB: Hopefully.

SOLO. COCKPIT OF A CHEROKEE 140. APRIL 1970.

DEB *is taxiing in a Cherokee 140, with* GARTH *the flying instructor.*

GARTH: Let's make this one a full stop Deb.

DEB *looks at her watch.*

DEB: I've still got twenty minutes left, Garth—

GARTH *begins to unbuckle his seat belt.*

GARTH: Remember to pull back at sixty knots.
DEB: Yeah, I did that.
GARTH: Your dad took much longer to get a handle on this stuff.

GARTH *opens the door and climbs out onto the wing. The propeller is loud. His hair blows in the wind.*

DEB: [*shouting*] What are you doing?!
GARTH: [*shouting*] Just make one circuit with a full stop landing!
DEB: [*shouting*] What?!
GARTH: [*shouting*] You know the drill.

GARTH *slams the door and climbs down to the tarmac and walks away.*

DEB: [*shouting*] Wait!!
GARTH: [*shouting*] You'll be fine!

DEB *is alone inside the aircraft. She takes a moment to assess this new reality.*

DEB: Ohmygod, ohmygod, ohmygod. Right. Fuck! It's happening.

DEB *takes a huge breath. She uses the following dialogue to calm herself. As she goes through what needs to be done—she hears* GARTH*'s voice in her head. She performs the actions as she speaks.*

/ Trim set. Master on. Mixture rich. Fuel on. Fuel pump on. Magnetos left and right checked. Flaps set. Instruments checked. Controls full and free. Harness and hatches secured.

GARTH: [*voiceover*] / Trim set. Master on. Mixture rich. Fuel on. Fuel pump on. Magnetos left and right checked. Flaps set. Instruments checked. Controls full and free. Harness and hatches secured.

DEB *speaks into her headset.*

DEB: Moorabbin Tower Delta Juliet Alpha ready.

DEB *hears a voice in her headset.*

AIR TRAFFIC CONTROLLER: Delta Juliet Alpha clear for take off.

DEB *takes a second to process this. She hears* GARTH*'s voice in her head.*

DEB: Okay. Deb, you're really doing this. You're on your own.

DEB *looks left and right.*

/ Check all clear of other aircraft. Line up.

GARTH: [*voiceover*] / Check all clear of other aircraft. Line up.

DEB *lines up the Cherokee on the runway.*

DEB: / Throttle set, airspeed increasing, keep straight with rudder, sixty knots, pull back gently.

GARTH: [*voiceover*] / Throttle set, airspeed increasing, keep straight with rudder, sixty knots, pull back gently.

DEB *feels the aircraft lift and her heart skips a beat.* DEB *laughs excitedly.* GARTH*'s voice drops out.*

DEB: Seventy knots. Climbing. Flaps up. Fuel pump off, turn, level off, attitude, trim. Just follow the circuit pattern.

DEB *enjoys herself as she completes the circuit. Then, realising what comes next, she takes a big breath.*

DEB: Okay. Okay. Now you gotta land it. There's no other option, Deb. Brakes off. Gear down and locked. Mixture rich. Fullest tank. Fuel on. Harness secure. Reduce speed. Commence descent. [*To herself*] Flap one. [*Into the headset*] Delta Juliet Alpha turning base, runway three-five right.

AIR TRAFFIC CONTROLLER: Delta Juliet Alpha.

DEB: [*to herself*] Flap two. [*Into the headset*] Delta Juliet Alpha turning final runway three-five right. [*To herself*] Full flap.

DEB *hears a voice in her headset.*

AIR TRAFFIC CONTROLLER: Delta Juliet Alpha cleared to land runway three-five right.

DEB: [*into the headset*] Cleared to land Delta Juliet Alpha. [*To herself*] Speed, speed, rate of descent. Flare. Power off. Hold off, hold off, hold off …

DEB *is at one with the airplane as she soars towards the landing strip and lands it perfectly.*

Wooooohoooooo!! I did it! I did it!!!

There's no better feeling. DEB*'s euphoric.*

ACT ONE

TIME JUMP: 1977

HELEN'S LAST FLIGHT. MELBOURNE AIRPORT LOUNGE. 1977.

'Help is on its Way' by Little River Band starts up.

*Ansett crew lounge. Three air hostesses—*MARGARET, PATRICIA *and* GLENDA*—stand, carry on bags over their shoulders, cigarettes in hand, fixing their make-up and hair. Soon another air hostess,* HELEN, *enters. As she approaches,* MARGARET *reaches into her carry on and pulls out a cupcake.* PATRICIA *stabs a candle into it and* GLENDA *lights it with her lighter.*

They begin to sing.

MARGARET / PATRICIA / GLENDA: Happy birth / day to—

HELEN: Stop! It's not a happy day. It's the last time we all fly together. I'm gonna miss you girls, so much.

HELEN *bursts into tears.* GLENDA *blows out the candle.*

PATRICIA: We're gonna to miss you too, Helen.

MARGARET: You've been like a sister to me.

GLENDA: Who'm I gonna bum smokes / off now?

HELEN: It's just so humiliating. Thirty-two and all washed-up! Fired from the job coz I'm too old?! Don't even have a husband as an excuse. What am I s'posed to do now?

GLENDA: Once you've waitressed in a test tube, Hels, you can waitress anywhere.

MARGARET: My cousin Penny could get you a job at Pizza Hut.

PATRICIA: Speaking of pizza, do you remember, Hels, at my first weigh-in you said, '*Stay off the pizza, Pat, no-one wants to be fired coz they're a pound overweight like Tall Jenny. So, eat air in the air, a grapefruit at port / and a piece of bacon as a last resort.*'

MARGARET / GLENDA: / ' ... *and a piece of bacon as a last resort.*'

MARGARET: That's a good / one.

GLENDA: I live / by that.

PATRICIA: Now, you can eat anything you want.

HELEN: S'pose you're right. I am very hungry.

HELEN *slowly pulls herself together. She blows her nose.*

GLENDA: And at least you worked as long as Mr Ansett let you. Any minute now, Hayden'll propose and *my* career will be over at twenty-two!

PATRICIA: And another thing, Hels, now you can have a root anytime you want without worrying you're gonna get fired for being up the duff.

MARGARET: Coz with Reg Ansett as your boss it'd be like coming clean to two dads.

HELEN: No chance of me getting up the duff, girls. I'm thirty-two! My period'll stop soon and I'll be a spinster. '*An old boiler*', like Reg says.

PATRICIA: Chin up / mate.

HELEN: Sexless, worthless, nothing.

HELEN *starts to sob again. The other women comfort her.*

MARGARET: No, no darl. You've got lovely skin.

PATRICIA: You make a wonderful pav.

GLENDA: You can tie a cherry stem with your tongue!

HELEN *pulls herself together. She blows her nose, then looks at each in turn.*

HELEN: Thanks Glenda, Patty, Marg. I'm a lucky old boiler to have girls like you.

They hug.

PATRICIA: You're not an old boiler, pet. You're a very attractive woman and you have a lovely speaking voice. Actually, you should consider receptionism.

GLENDA: Every man needs a good receptionist.

HELEN *stifles a little sob.*

MARGARET: Now, be cheery, Hels.

PATRICIA: You gotta pull yourself together for your *last* flight.

GLENDA: And remember what they said at stewardess school? '*A smile does more for your face / than make-up does.*'

MARGARET / PATRICIA / HELEN: —*'than make-up does.'*

Beat.

GLENDA: But make-up's still really important.

I MADE A HORSE. ROYAL VICTORIAN AERO CLUB. MOORABBIN. 1977.

'Living in the 70's' by Skyhooks plays loud.

As DEB*—twenty-three, tall, striking and audacious—sits at a table locked in a fierce arm wrestle with* TODD*—weaselly, with a voice built to annoy;* RICHARD*—well mannered and kind;* KENNETH*—old-school, accidental chauvinist; and* BRUCE*—no-frills man of his time, cheer* DEB *on.*

RICHARD / BRUCE: Deb! Deb! Deb! Deb! Deb!
KENNETH: C'mon, Toddy!
TODD: Shut up idiots! You're throwing me off my game.
KENNETH: Ya not gonna cry, are ya?
TODD: Shush! I'm concentrating.

DEB *and* TODD *are locked into each other's eyes. Faces red. Lips pursed. Their arms teeter left then right, then left and right. With one final push,* DEB *eases* TODD*'s arm to the table.*

DEB: Woohoo! Gotcha!
BRUCE: Bad luck, Toddy! Girl's on top today.
KENNETH: Your shout, mate!
TODD: Really?
KENNETH: Them's the rules.
TODD: This is bullshit. You all know how hungover / I am.
DEB: / Excuses, excuses, Todd. If you can fly a plane after a bender, which we all know you do …
KENNETH / RICHARD: We all do.
TODD: I'm just not full bottle today.
DEB: What you want me to do, add weights round my neck? I'm not bloody Phar Lap.

The guys laugh at TODD.

BRUCE: Don't worry, Todd, it's a rite of passage to be beaten by Debbie.

DEB: Who's next?

RICHARD: You should be in bed. School teachers shouldn't be up past eleven on a school night.

DEB: Don't try'n get out of it, Richie.

DEB *gets her arm ready.*

C'mon!

KENNETH: Why do you have to make everything a competition, Deb?

DEB: I don't have to, Ken. I like to.

RICHARD: You racing in the Freda Thompson this weekend?

DEB: You bet!

TODD: The Freda what?

KENNETH: The ladies' aerial race / around Port Phillip Bay.

RICHARD: Round Port Phillip / Bay.

DEB: I'm gonna win it this year.

KENNETH: Go get the drinks / Todd.

TODD *heads off.*

DEB: You should come along, Richie. Bring the new Air Traffic Control guy.

RICHARD: Pete Wardley?

DEB: Do you know him?

RICHARD: Only by reputation.

DEB: What have you heard?

BRUCE: I heard he likes the ladies.

DEB: Hope so. Otherwise it'd be a bit of a waste! Apparently he's gonna be at Brad P's Fondue party Friday but if he doesn't get there—you gotta bring him to the race, okay?

DEB *puts her elbow back on the table.*

C'mon?

RICHARD: Don't wanna kill your winning streak.

DEB: Bruce?

BRUCE: Gotta call it a night.

BRUCE *gets up.*

I start ground training at Ansett in the morning.

BRUCE *exits.* TODD *returns with the drinks.*

DEB: That's right, I forgot to tell you, Richie, I applied.
KENNETH: To Ansett?
DEB: And TAA.
TODD: To be a Hostie?

TODD *puts a drink in front of* DEB.

DEB: Bugger off, Todd.
TODD: I dunno if they'd be lookin' for lady pilots, Deb.
DEB: For your information, Todd, a few years back my dad organised for me to meet the general manager—
TODD: Frank Pascoe.
DEB: And he said that once I got my ducks in a row, I should apply. So I did.
KENNETH: Pascoe doesn't own the company, Deb.
TODD: At Ansett, Sir Reg is God.
DEB: If he's God he already knows I'm a better pilot than you guys.
BRUCE: Ooooh.
KENNETH: Ouch.
TODD: Owwww.
RICHARD: That may be true, Debbie, but it doesn't mean he'll say yes.

Beat.

DEB: When I was a kid, more than anything, I wanted a horse. But my parents said '*No Deb, you can't have a horse. We're in North Balwyn. We don't have the bloody room.*' So you know what I did?
RICHARD: What did you do, Debbie?
DEB: I made a horse. With some boxes, a mop and a plank of wood. It wasn't pretty and it certainly wasn't comfortable. But I got my horse.

Silence.

TODD: I think I zoned out for a minute, what's the homemade horse got to do with anything?
RICHARD: She doesn't take no for an answer.

FIRST KISS. AIR TRAFFIC CONTROL TOWER. 1977.

Night-time. The sound of a storm. Thunder and lightning.

PETER WARDLEY *records on ATIS.*

PETER: Moorabbin Terminal information November. Airport is closed to all *visual* departures and arrivals. *Instrument* departure and arrivals only. Wind three one zero, three five knots, visibility six thousand metres in rain, temperature one eight, Q, N, H one zero one three, Moorabbin November.

The phone rings. PETER *answers it.*

Peter Wardley speaking. Oh, Debbie. Pete Wardley speaking. Sure, the storms not passing in a hurry, yeah, come on up.

Smiling, PETER *hangs up and readies himself. A beat later,* DEB *enters sheepishly. They greet awkwardly. The chemistry is palpable.*

You making tower visits, now?

DEB: Never been up before. I wanted to see the view.

DEB *looks out at the storm.*

I had a really great time the other night.

PETER: Did you, now?

DEB: Told Mum how I beat you in darts. She said I was gonna scare you off.

PETER: I don't scare easily.

DEB: Well, you didn't run away when I lost the air race.

PETER: You came third!

DEB: Didn't win though.

Beat.

PETER: What else did you say to your mum about me?

DEB: That you weren't really the marrying kind, but I'd probably marry you anyway.

PETER *smiles.*

PETER: Been there, done that.

DEB: Yeah, but that sounds like it was just a … practice run.

PETER *smiles.* DEB *picks up the binoculars from the table, puts the strap around her neck and looks out the window.* PETER *approaches from behind, puts his hands over hers and manoeuvres her so that she's facing the carpark.*

PETER: Lately, I've been using these to see when your v-dub turns up in the carpark.

DEB: You've been spying on me, Peter Wardley?

PETER: More keeping an eye out. I was looking for you every day this week till Richie told me you don't just teach blokes to fly—you teach at a high school too.

DEB: That's right.

PETER: So you keep yourself pretty busy, Miss Lawrie.

PETER *smiles.*

Yeah, I keep myself busy too. I collect stamps, do a bit of archery. I dabble in tropical fish tanks. It's very tricky to regulate the temperature of the water. I bake. Lately, I've been thinking about getting into the restaurant game. Anyway, what about you? D'you like teaching?

DEB: I don't mind it.

Beat.

But I was standing on the oval at lunch duty the other day when a jet flew over and I thought, that'll be Bruce in six months' time … I want it to be me.

PETER: Well, you seem like the kind of girl who gets what she wants.

They look at each other. It gets steamy. DEB *breaks off.*

DEB: If I can just get an interview with one of the airlines—I know I'll get in.

PETER: Pretty confident, aren't you?

DEB: Well, I'm pretty good.

PETER: That's what all the blokes say. You've got quite the reputation.

DEB: So have you.

PETER *smiles at her cheekiness. Beat.*

PETER: Why do you think you're so good?

DEB: I've done a lot of flying.

PETER: You're twenty-three.

DEB: Yeah, but I knew getting my hours up was the only way I'd ever have a career in aviation. So every chance I get, I fly. During uni, my boyfriend and I'd chuck our mates in the back of a coupla six-seaters and go on flying safaris through the outback.

PETER: Seriously?

DEB: Yeah, we'd cover hundreds and hundreds of miles every trip.

PETER: But it's more than that. When I saw you race last week … you don't fly like everyone else.

DEB: I guess that's coz I— … you know that saying; 'Flying by the seat of your pants?'

PETER: Yeah.

DEB: It actually comes from flying. At some point, if you're lucky, it's like … like you and the aircraft become … one. You don't fly using only *knowledge*, you … fly by feel.

PETER: Go on.

DEB: It's like how a race car driver knows how far to push a car, or if you listen to certain musicians they become the instrument … That's flying for me. I don't just use pieces of myself like in the rest of my life. When I fly, I use all of me. And it doesn't matter what's happening down here on the ground. Up there, I'm completely in control and completely free at the same time.

Beat.

Does that make sense?

PETER *looks at* DEB *with admiration. He leans in. They kiss.*

LORRAINE COOPER. ROYAL VICTORIAN AERO CLUB. MOORABBIN. 1977.

A confused and annoyed DEB *stands with* RICHARD, KENNETH *and* TODD.

DEB: Six times I've applied to Ansett! It's always the same. ' *... you will not be advancing to the interview stage at this time. Keep us up to date with any changes in flying hours.*'

It makes no sense. My hours are way better than any of yours were. But they wouldn't ask me to keep them updated if they weren't interested. Right?

Beat.

Right?

RICHARD: They're *not* interested, Deb.

Beat.

I heard from Bruce they're hoping you'll go the way of Lorraine Cooper.

DEB: Which way's that?

RICHARD: She applied in seventy-four, interviewed in seventy-five, got put on a waiting list for two years and last month, on her twenty-seventh birthday, she was bumped off the list coz she 'exceeded the maximum entry age.' But at least she got an interview. Which is more than Beryl Young ever got.

TODD: That bird's personal pilot to Sir Joh Bjelke-Petersen, isn't she? She'd be happy as Larry.

DEB: How would you know?

KENNETH: You're a great instructor, Deb, but no-one's gonna put you in charge of a 727.

DEB: Why not?

TODD: You could run a charter company / or …

DEB: I don't want to run a charter company, I want to be a commercial / airline pilot!

KENNETH: Stick to the small planes, Debbie.

DEB: I want to command the big / ones.

KENNETH: That's unrealistic.

DEB: How is it unrealistic, Ken? People I *taught* to fly are now airline pilots.

KENNETH: I don't think women are built to fly the big jets / there I said it!

DEB: I'm better built / than you are.

KENNETH: And obviously Ansett feels the same!

Beat. DEB *is hurt, then enraged.*

DEB: I will not settle for less than the rest of you.

SHE'S A BIRD. ANSETT BOARDROOM. 1978.

Dutch head of intake, CAPTAIN HENRY THEUNISSEN, *sits at a boardroom table with* CAPTAIN TOMLIN *and* CAPTAIN BURNETT. FRANK PASCOE *hands* HENRY *a piece of paper.*

FRANK: Here's his application, Henry. His qualifications are not spectacular but his wife's expecting and Reg is good mates with his father, so he'd like you to get the boy in for an interview.

HENRY: If you say so.

HENRY *shuffles through more applications.*

And what about this one? Perhaps I have lost something in translation, but it says here this is the tenth time this pilot's applied?

CAPTAIN TOMLIN: Qualifications?

HENRY: Exemplary.

CAPTAIN BURNETT: Education?

HENRY: Bachelor of Science in Maths, Physics and Chemistry. Specialising in Nuclear and Upper Atmosphere Physics and Pure Maths. If anything, he's overqualified.

CAPTAIN TOMLIN: What's the name?

HENRY: Lawrie.

They all laugh, except HENRY.

Am I missing something?

FRANK: No, no, no. Lawrie's a bird.

HENRY: A bird?

Beat.

Perhaps something has been lost in translation?

CAPTAIN BURNETT: She's a girl, Henry.

HENRY: Well, she's very impressive.

FRANK: Nice lass, too. Met her a few years back when her father set up a little meeting for her. But it's not going to happen. Reg is dead-set on not having lady pilots in the airline.

CAPTAIN TOMLIN: They're not cut out for it.

HENRY: Women have been flying commercially in the US since seventy-three. And there's a number of female jet pilots in Europe.

CAPTAIN BURNETT: Yeah, but we do things differently down under, Henry.

FRANK: Our pilots can fly till they're sixty and, like Reg says, you wouldn't want your grandma flying a plane.

HENRY: Actually, my grandmother did fly a plane.

Beat.

FRANK: Either way, Henry, Reg won't budge on this.

HENRY: Right. Well, the poor girl's twenty-four years old. She doesn't need to spend the next few years chasing a dream that's never going to happen. Let's bring her in so we can cross her off the list.

FIRST HURDLE. MUM'S HOUSE. 1978.

PETER, MUM *and* DEB *sit at the dinner table. The wine is as free-flowing as the conversation. It's* PETER *and* MUM*'s first meeting and* DEB*'s buzzing, having just returned from her first Ansett interview.*

MUM: So, there was only one Captain at the interview, Debbie?

DEB: It was a pre-interview, Mum. So the Captain just went through my logbook, checked my hours were legit, made sure there were no gaps. He seemed really impressed with all the flying I'd done.

MUM: Well, those safaris—

DEB: And going back and forth to Quilpie.

MUM: Don't remind me!

PETER: Where's Quilpie?

MUM: Exactly, Peter. It's a Queensland town in the middle of nowhere. And eighty miles *outside* that town on an abandoned sheep station—

DEB: Cattle / station.

MUM: —was a mine. And at twenty years of age, my daughter thought she should be the one to ferry opals out of it.

DEB: They were actually boulders with opals inside / them.

MUM: For some criminal / whose name was …

DEB: He wasn't a criminal Mum, he was a Melbourne / jeweller.

MUM: Whose name was Johnny Mules.

PETER: To be fair, Johnny Mules does sound like a criminal.

MUM: Thank you / Peter—

DEB: He was a friend of Dad's.

MUM: Considering who your father hangs out with these days that brought me no comfort.

There were no airstrips, no phones, no hospitals if anything went wrong.

DEB: Nothing went wrong / Mum.

MUM: And this man on a motorbike, who ran the mine, didn't even want Debbie there.

DEB: He'd never seen a girl fly a plane before.

MUM: And you had to stay in that hovel. No sheets on the beds, no food in the fridge, frogs in the dunny.

DEB: Motorbike guy could barely look at me, day one. But on day two Johnny Mules sent us on a recce together. I flew the plane, motorbike guy was in charge of surveying.

MUM: Coz there were no *maps* of the area. Can you imagine / Peter?

DEB: And he realised pretty quickly he needed me if he wanted to get back.

MUM: And up there, she proved herself.

DEB: I must have, coz the next time I flew in he put a roast in the oven and sheets on the bed.

MUM: And you were touched by that, weren't you, Debbie?

DEB: I won his respect.

Embarrassed by revealing too much, DEB *gets up to clear the plates.*

MUM: What did your father say about you finally getting an interview?

DEB: He doesn't know.

MUM: I thought he'd be the first you'd tell.

DEB: I'd have to see to him to tell him. And Lady Macbeth keeps him on a tight rein.

DEB *exits with plates. Beat.*

MUM: Debbie was her father's shadow.

PETER: Really?

MUM: Followed him everywhere. She'd sit in his office till all hours. He was a patent attorney and she'd help him sort through his files. At uni she studied the same thing he did. She was only interested in flying because he was. If she gets any further with this Ansett business he's the only one she'll want to share it with. But history suggests he'll disappoint. Which means she'll just be stuck with me. And I don't know the first thing about flying.

PETER: Don't worry, Dorothy, I know a fair bit about it and I'm planning on sticking round.

DEB *re-enters.*

MUM: So you think you'll get a second interview, Debbie?

DEB: Yeah I do.

PETER *holds up his glass.*

PETER: To Future First Officer Lawrie.

DEB *grabs her glass and they cheers.*

MUM: I hope you're right. But don't get your hopes up, Debbie; no Australian airlines have female pilots yet.

DEB: Then I'll be the first.

SELECTION PANEL. ANSETT BOARDROOM. SECOND INTERVIEW. 1978.

CAPTAIN HENRY THEUNISSEN, CAPTAIN TOMLIN, CAPTAIN BURNETT *and* CAPTAIN BALL *interview* DEB. *It's serious.*

HENRY: De'boora you are one of twenty-nine candidates being granted a *second* interview for the July intake. Ultimately, only fourteen trainees will be chosen.

DEB: Right.

HENRY: Successful applicants will be those with the highest scores determined by the selection panel here today. Each panelist will give each candidate an aggregate score out of a hundred: based on age, educational and flying qualifications and motivation. If we all agree you have the potential to be in the programme, you'll undergo a psychological appraisal. Is that clear, De'boora?

DEB: Crystal.

HENRY: I think something has been lost in translation?

DEB: I'm clear.

HENRY: Good.

The interrogation begins.

CAPTAIN BURNETT: First things first, Miss Lawrie, if you're accepted into the programme, what do you intend to wear?

Beat.

DEB: I beg your pardon?

CAPTAIN TOMLIN: There's no *female* uniform.

CAPTAIN BURNETT: How're you going to go wearing one of ours?

DEB: Well I'm not crazy about the front pleat, but I'll make it work.

HENRY *smiles. The* CAPTAINS *titter.*

CAPTAIN BALL: What about those?

DEB: My ears?

CAPTAIN TOMLIN: Your earrings.

CAPTAIN BURNETT: They could pose a threat.

DEB: How so?

CAPTAIN BALL: In emergency landings, the pilot has to open the side window and climb down a rope.
What if they get caught?

DEB: On what?

CAPTAIN BALL: The rope?

CAPTAIN TOMLIN: The window?

CAPTAIN BURNETT: Anything.

All the CAPTAINS *stare at her intently. Beat.* DEB *removes her sleepers and rests them on the table.*

DEB: I wasn't born with them.

The CAPTAINS *make notes.*

CAPTAIN BURNETT: Should you make Captain, how will your co-pilots react to getting orders from a lady?

DEB: If I'm Captain, I assume they'll follow them.

CAPTAIN BALL: And what about the public? They're used to women looking pretty and serving them nuts. How will they feel when a woman's voice comes over the PA?

CAPTAIN TOMLIN: [*a high-pitched girlie voice*] '*Hello this is your Lady Captain / speaking.*'

CAPTAIN BURNETT: It might be a source of great anxiety for them.

CAPTAIN TOMLIN: What will they be thinking?

DEB: I can't pretend to know what they'll be thinking. All I can do is get them to their destination as smoothly and safely as possible. Something I've been doing on every flight I've piloted since I was seventeen years old.

The CAPTAINS, *impressed, all write.*

CAPTAIN BALL: Do you have a boyfriend, Miss Lawrie?

DEB: I just got engaged.

HENRY: Congrat / ulations.

CAPTAIN TOMLIN: When's the big day?

DEB: We haven't decided.

CAPTAIN BALL: Then we should talk about the elephant in the room.

DEB: Which elephant?

CAPTAIN BALL: Babies.

CAPTAIN TOMLIN: When will you have them?

DEB: Haven't thought about it.

CAPTAIN BALL: Come on, every little girl dreams of being a mother.

DEB: Do they?

CAPTAIN BALL: You know they do.

CAPTAIN TOMLIN: How many kids are you having?

CAPTAIN BURNETT: I've always thought three's a / good number.

CAPTAIN TOMLIN: The third just takes care of itself.

HENRY: Let Miss Lawrie answer the question, gentlemen.

DEB: I don't know …

CAPTAIN BALL: You must have some idea.

DEB: … One, maybe two max.

CAPTAIN BALL: Which is it?

CAPTAIN BURNETT: You need to make a decision.

HENRY: She said one or two, gentlemen.

CAPTAIN BURNETT: And how do you plan to look after them?

DEB: I'll have a husband. He'll help me do it.

Beat.

CAPTAIN BALL / TOMLIN / BURNETT No, seriously.

DEB: I don't know, but I don't see it as a hurdle.

CAPTAIN BURNETT: It's just not in Ansett's best interest to invest time and money into training someone who's gonna run off and have four or five / kids—

DEB: I never said / four or five—

CAPTAIN BALL: How are you s'posed to be a great pilot if you spend your days breastfeeding?

CAPTAIN BURNETT: Ironing?

CAPTAIN TOMLIN: Making school lunches?

DEB: All I know is I intend to fly whether I have kids / or not.

CAPTAIN BURNETT: The best laid plans are paved with good intention Miss Lawrie, but where young ladies are involved they often / go awry.

CAPTAIN BALL: You flip and flop and change your mind. I mean, that's your nature. Can you really see yourself in this industry for a *lifetime*, / Miss Lawrie?

CAPTAIN BURNETT: Or is this something you have a little go at then walk away / from?

CAPTAIN BALL: You're sure you're not just dabbling?

DEB: Dabbling? Flying is my life. And I intend to make it my career! The fact I'm a woman has nothing to do with it. I consider myself a pilot!

Beat.

You won't find anyone more dedicated, anyone more professional or anyone more committed. And if you employ me as a pilot with Ansett, I promise I will not let you down.

The CAPTAINS *all look pretty impressed, by and large. Nods and notes all round.* HENRY *stands.*

HENRY: You're extremely skilled and very passionate, De'boora, that seems clear. You'll be hearing from us in due course.

DEB: Thank you.

DEB *exits.* HENRY *turns back to the men.*

CAPTAIN BALL: I don't mind her.

CAPTAIN BURNETT: We've hired less qualified men.

CAPTAIN TOMLIN: With less experience.

HENRY: If she gets through the psychological appraisal I don't see how we *can't* offer her a traineeship.

MARY CALLS. MUM'S HOUSE. 1977. NIGHT.

DEB *and* MUM *in the lounge with tea and biscuits.* Countdown *plays in the background.*

The phone rings.

MUM: Turn it down, Deb.

DEB *turns down the TV.* MUM *picks up the phone.*

Dorothy Barnes speaking?

Spotlight comes up on MARY PERRETT*—fifty-five, fun and gossipy—on the phone.*

MARY: Hello Dorothy, it's Mary Perrett here. I have some exciting news I thought you could pass on to your Debbie.

MUM: She's here right now. Do you want to speak to her?

MARY: I shouldn't really … but yes, yes put her on.

MUM: Debbie, Mary Perrett wants to speak to you.

DEB: [*mouthing*] Who?

MUM *covers the phone.*

MUM: Mary Perrett. I play tennis with her every Wednesday.

MUM *thrusts the phone at* DEB.

DEB: Hello?

MARY: Hello Deborah? It's Mary Perrett here, I play tennis with your mother every Wednesday.

DEB: Right. Hello Mary.

MARY: I just had a bit of news I wanted to share. I don't know if you know but I work at a place called Chandler Macleod and we do the independent psychological testing for all the Ansett trainee pilots.

MUM: [*whispering*] What's she / saying?

DEB: [*covering the phone*] Shush!

MARY: I'm sure you know Dorothy's very proud of you and she mentioned, more than once, that you were going through the interview process there at Ansett. Once I knew that, well, I thought I'd keep a little eye out / for your results.

MUM: [*whispering*] What's she saying?

DEB: [*covering the phone*] Please Mum, I'm trying to listen! [*Back to* MARY.] Sorry, Mary, go on.

MARY: Anyway, I arrived at work today and there was a bit of a buzz in the air because one set of results belonged to a '*woman*'. In all the time I've been at the company we've never had a woman get this far. And I thought / well, it had to be you.

MUM: What's / happening?!

DEB: [*covering the phone*] Mum!

MARY: Anyway, when all the interest had died down I had a little peek at your scores.

Beat.

DEB: Aaand?

MARY: This is completely confidential, obviously.

DEB: Obviously.

MARY: They're bloody good, love. They're better than good, they're great. You held your own against nearly thirty men. And you had the *third highest* score!

DEB: Third highest?

MUM: Third highest?!

MARY: Third out of twenty-nine! And you've been placed in the *highly recommended* category!

DEB: Oh my god. Oh my / god.

MARY: Dorothy said your wedding's coming up in January?

DEB: Yeah that's right.

MARY: Well, you better get your honeymoon out of the way. Because it looks like, come July, you'll be training to be an Ansett pilot!

DEB *stands beaming. Speechless. Beat.*

DEB: I don't know what to say.

MARY: Don't say anything, Deb, because it's a secret.

DEB: Got it, got it, got it. Thank you so much for letting me know, Mary.

MARY: My pleasure. Mum's the word!

MARY *hangs up. Lights out on* MARY. DEB *hangs up the phone and looks to* MUM.

MUM: Did you get in?

DEB: I think so!

MUM: Oh, Debbie! You did it!!

MUM *and* DEB *squeal.*

REG-ECTED. DEB AND PETE'S LOUNGE ROOM. 1978.

DEB *sits on the couch reading a magazine.* PETER, *in work attire carrying a pile of mail, bursts through the front door. He holds out an envelope to her.*

PETER: From Ansett, DL.

DEB *grabs the envelope, rips it open, hardly able to contain her excitement. She pulls out a piece of paper and starts to read.*

DEB: '*Dear Miss Lawrie ... we regret to inform you ... that you ... did not make the final selection.*'

DEB*'s been hit for six. She screws it up in a tight ball and throws it over her shoulder.*

Fuck 'em.

PETER *puts down the rest of the mail, picks up the piece of paper, unfurls it and reads.*

PETER: ' *... you will not be considered for any subsequent trainee pilot intakes ...* ' That's such bullshit, Deb.

DEB: They don't want me.

PETER: They've rejected you coz you're a woman.

DEB: D'ya reckon?!

PETER: They need to reconsider.

DEB: Great idea! Do you want to call them or should I?

DEB *turns to leave.*

PETER: Hang on, hang on … wait, wait, wait! I read something in the paper yesterday …

PETER *runs over to grab the newspaper sitting on the table and rifles through it.*

About this new Act the Victorian Government / passed.

DEB: I don't care, Pete!

DEB *starts to leave again.*

PETER: Deb, wait! … Here it is … ' … *The Equal Opportunity Act* … ' It says '*It is unlawful for an employer to discriminate against a person on the grounds of sex ... by refusing to offer employment.*'

DEB: So?

PETER: So, they've created a *Board* to deal with this exact situation.

DEB: Well, if there's a magical board …

PETER: We should contact them!

DEB: No.

PETER: But what Ansett's doing is now *against the law*!

DEB: Ansett's a private bloody company Pete, they can do what they want.

PETER: But that's the thing Deb, I don't think they can.

Beat.

You were in the top three!!

DEB: I know that, Peter.

Beat.

PETER: But they don't know that we know that!

Beat. DEB *goes to head off again.*

DEB: I don't want to work for them / anyway.

PETER: Yes, you do!

DEB: No, I don't!

PETER: Yes, you do! You're too good a pilot not to fight this, DL!

DEB *is quietened.*

PETER: Just think about it.

BICCIES. EQUAL OPPORTUNITY OFFICE. 1978.

DEB *and* PETER *sit opposite* FAY MARLES *at the Equal Opportunity office. A plate of biccies sit between them. She casts her eyes across a number of documents.*

FAY: I'm Fay Marles. My job as Commissioner is to listen to your complaint and ascertain whether your claim has validity. If I deem it does, I'll conduct interviews, gather evidence, then attempt a conciliation with the other party.

PETER: Good luck with that, Fay.

FAY: If conciliation fails but I believe you have a case, I'll refer your complaint to the Board.

DEB: Okay.

FAY: Just a heads up, there's been seventy-one claimants so far and none of them have made it to the Board. No point testing the law if we don't think there's at least a chance of winning.

DEB: Well if it doesn't work, it doesn't work. I'm only here coz he dragged me.

> FAY *nods, grabs a biscuit from the table and takes a bite before offering one to* DEB *and* PETER.

FAY: Milk Arrowroot?

DEB: No, thanks.

PETER: I'm right.

FAY: Mmm. Yum. So, Deborah, explain to me why you think you've been discriminated against.

> DEB *is silent as she tries to find the words.*

PETER: It's obvious. She's a bloody great pilot, better than a bunch of guys they've employed.

FAY: Okay. But I imagine it's very competitive.

PETER: You won't find anyone more competitive than DL.

FAY: Thank you, Peter. If I could just hear from Deborah. What led you to believe you were better than the chosen applicants?

DEB: I know I'm just as good. My flying record's spotless, I've got sixteen hundred flying hours / under my belt—

PETER: All you / need is five hundred.

DEB: —and a number of the pilots I *trained* are now working for Ansett.

FAY: Really?

> FAY *notes this down.*

But what makes you think your rejection was based on gender?

PETER: None of the blokes got asked how many babies they were planning on having.

FAY: They asked you that?

DEB: Yep. Wasn't it a waste to train me if I was just going to run off to be a mother? Who was gonna look after them? I tried to tell them it wouldn't be an issue. But they wouldn't believe me. Eventually, I just said Pete would help out.

PETER: Did you?

DEB: Well, if you end up going with that / restaurant idea.

FAY: It certainly sounds like your gender came into play but that doesn't *prove* that the pilots hired in July simply weren't better candidates. And if we can't prove it—there would be no point advancing your case to court.

DEB *and* PETER *are silent.*

PETER: Tell her.

DEB: I don't want to get anyone in trouble.

PETER: Go on, Deb.

Beat.

DEB: You only get a first interview with a commercial airline if you meet all the requirements.

FAY: Okay.

DEB: You get a second if your CV lines up and your log book's consistent.

FAY: Alright.

DEB: And you only get to the third / stage—

PETER: The psychological appraisal.

DEB: —if you answer all the Captains' questions and concerns in that second interview. So pilots who advance to that third stage are kind of on an even playing field.

FAY: Uh-huh.

DEB: My mum knows a woman who works at Chandler Macleod.

PETER: The place that does the psych testing—

DEB: —and this woman calls out of the blue coz she'd seen my results and she told me I was third-highest.

PETER: And was put in the Highly Recommend category.

DEB: So you tell me, if there are fourteen places up for grabs, and I came in third, how can I *not* be offered a job?

UNSAFE. REG ANSETT'S OFFICE. 1978.

The lights come up on REG ANSETT*—sixty-nine years old—on a phone in his office. He is talking to* FAY *in her office, who has him on speaker so she can take notes.*

REG: Whilst it's my personal belief women should not be commercial airline pilots, Mrs Marles, Ansett did not *discriminate* against this woman.

FAY: But, it is your personal belief, Sir Ansett?

REG: They're big machines Mrs Marles, a woman's not strong enough to handle them if, say, the hydraulics fail.

FAY: I didn't realise my survival in an emergency depends on my pilot's musculature.

REG: They must be strong, of course.

FAY: You test for strength then?

REG: … No.

FAY *notes this.*

FAY: Then how do you determine how strong your pilots are?

REG: It's implied, isn't it?

FAY: Is it?

Silence.

Were there other factors that contributed to your rejection of Miss Lawrie?

REG: The Union won't have it.

FAY: You think there'd be industrial action?

REG: I'm sure of it.

FAY *notes that down.*

FAY: And is there anything else you'd like me to take into consideration as I make my decision?

REG: Your decision?

REG *scoffs.*

You can't have someone who goes hysterical once a month fly a plane.

For a moment, FAY *is speechless.*

FAY: '*Hysterical. Once a month*?'

REG: During their monthlies.

FAY: I understand the allusion you're making to the female menstrual cycle, Mr Ansett, but what makes you think Deborah Lawrie has any issue with hers? Was that covered in the application?

REG: Don't be stupid.

FAY: I can assure you, Mr Ansett, I'm not stupid. Merely trying to ascertain the facts.

REG: The fact is women shouldn't fly commercial aircraft.

FAY: Why?

REG: It's not safe.

FAY: What is it about women, Mr Ansett, that you find so dangerous?

Beat. REG *hangs up.*

Mr Ansett?

FAY *hangs up. They've got a case.*

FLY GIRL. ANSETT 747. IN THE GALLEY. 1978.

GLENDA *stands smoking in the galley of an airplane, on a break after the dinner service.*

BRUCE: [*voiceover*] Ladies and gentlemen, this is your First Officer, Bruce Woodbridge, speaking. We've reached our cruising altitude of thirty-five-thousand feet. We are anticipating some turbulence up ahead, so please remain seated with your seatbelts fastened. Our cabin crew are available to assist you with any further needs.

The lights dim. PATRICIA *enters, bends down and looks in a low cupboard.*

PATRICIA: Where are all the rice puddings gone?

GLENDA: Those kids in business have had half a dozen each.

PATRICIA: They're the ones asking! Bugger 'em. Can I bum a smoke, Glen?

GLENDA: Sure thing, Pat.

GLENDA *offers* PATRICIA *her cigarette box. She lights up.*

PATRICIA: What's news?

GLENDA: Helen started her new job, Monday. Receptionist at an ad company on Collins Street. You were right, they said she had a lovely speaking voice.

MARGARET *comes racing in, conspiratorially.*

MARGARET: Excellent, you're both here, I've got some really good goss.

GLENDA *hands* MARGARET *a smoke and lights it.*

Have you heard about the girl trying to fly the plane?

GLENDA: Which girl?

PATRICIA: What plane?

MARGARET: The girl who wants to be an Ansett pilot.

GLENDA: That's impossible.

MARGARET: No, she went through the interviews, did all the tests and apparently was as good as any bloke but they rejected her. So she might be taking Reg Ansett to court!

PATRICIA: You don't say?

GLENDA: My Hayden says girls should keep away from all things mechanical, else they'll get hurt.

PATRICIA: Glenda, Hayden's easy on the eye but he's what the feminists are calling a chauvinist.

MARGARET: That's the second time I've heard that word this week. When we landed in Brissie yesterday, I heard Kerry shout at Captain Spencer, '*You're a male chauvinist pig, Simon!*'

GLENDA: Was Captain Spencer okay?

PATRICIA: If it was Captain Spencer, he no doubt deserved it.

GLENDA: I just don't think it's nice to get into name-calling.

MARGARET: He pinched her on the bum!

GLENDA: A pinch on the bum's part of the job. When it happens to me, I just clench my buttocks and think of a rainforest.

PATRICIA: No offence, Glen, but you need to get onto Gloria Steinem. S-T-E-I-N-E-M. I read an article by her in the *Women's Weekly*. Very illuminating.

GLENDA: Hayden says I shouldn't read, it'll give me wrinkles.

PATRICIA: Hayden's got a lot of opinions.

MARGARET: He definitely wouldn't be into that girl trying to fly the plane.

GLENDA: Are they going to let her?

The three women start to sway.

BRUCE: [*voiceover*] Ladies and gentlemen, this is your First Officer speaking. We are experiencing some turbulence, please ensure your seatbelts are securely fastened.

The women, now swaying a little more, expertly put everything not pinned down into the cupboards and drawers.

MARGARET: Apparently Reg says she'll never be allowed to fly because her period makes her hysterical.

GLENDA: Makes sense. After her thirteenth kid, my nan's periods went all over the shop and *she* went hysterical. They had to give her a lobotomy.

MARGARET: Geez Glen, that's a nightmare!

PATRICIA: I bet all she needed was a bloody nap.

The turbulence gets so bad they all get into their seats and do up their seatbelts. Click.

GLENDA: She must be a lesbian.

PATRICIA: Who?

GLENDA: Fly Girl. Coz if lesbians want to be men, they probably want to do men's jobs too.

PATRICIA: Lesbians don't want to be men, darl.

GLENDA: How do you know?

PATRICIA: I'm considering being one myself.

MARGARET: You don't say?

The turbulence subsides. Beat.

PATRICIA: Well, I hope she makes it.

GLENDA: Who?

MARGARET: / Fly Girl.

PATRICIA: Fly Girl. I hope they let her fly. Imagine, a woman up there at the front.

They look to the front of the plane and try to imagine it. Beat.

MARGARET: Wouldn't that be something.

RICHARD'S 'I GOT INTO TAA' DRINKS. AEROCLUB. 1978.

DEB, PETER, KENNETH *and* RICHARD *celebrate at the Aeroclub;* RICHARD*'s TAA uniform is hanging on his chair.*

DEB: Another reason Reg cited for not employing me was the Union'd kick up a stink. So Fay calls the Exec Director there at the Federation of Air Pilots—

KENNETH: Len Coysh, / great bloke.

DEB: —and he says the Union would have no problem with me.

PETER: Fay tells Ansett that—

DEB: —and a week later they send her a letter saying I *was* judged on my merits but wasn't good enough to get in!

PETER: Next thing Fay calls and says, / '*There's no doubt in my mind, you've got a case.*'

DEB: / '*You've got a case.*'

PETER: And we're gonna fight it all the way.

RICHARD: Looks like you've got yourself a new project, Pete?

DEB: I really like Fay. She's smart, super organised, gets shit done. She's like a one-man band.

> DEB *stands, grabs* RICHARD*'s uniform and starts to put his oversized shirt on.*

RICHARD: A one woman / band.

DEB: Exactly.

> DEB *puts on* RICHARD*'s oversized TAA hat.*

RICHARD: What are you doing, Deb?

DEB: Practising. How do I look?

> DEB *does a twirl.*

KENNETH: It's not very flattering.

PETER: Don't listen to Ken—you look hot.

> DEB *ties the shirt at the waist to make it look better.*

RICHARD: Debbie don't crease it, I don't want to iron it / again.

> DEB *holds up her glass and makes a toast.*

DEB: Shush. To Richard. For getting into TAA.

PETER / KENNETH: To Richard!!

They all cheers.

RICHARD: You'll be next, Deb.

TRISH—*smart, neat, a little bit pregnant—walks in and waves at* DEB.

DEB: Won't be a minute, Trish.

TRISH: Lesson isn't for another ten, I'm early.

DEB: Sit down!

TRISH *sits at the table.*

PETER: Fay reckons Deb's case'll be the first real test of this new Discrimination Law.

TRISH: Oh, so they're taking you to the Equal Opportunity Board, Deb?

PETER: Yep.

DEB: It won't be a big deal.

TRISH: If Fay Marles is backing you to be their first case it's coz she thinks you can win. Which would be a big deal.

PETER: Yeah, Fay reckons it could really snowball.

KENNETH: You'll be famous, / Debbie.

DEB: Hope not. How embarrass / ing.

KENNETH: Do you go to this *Equal Opportunity* place on your own?

PETER: It's a court, dickhead. She'll have a legal team.

RICHARD: Got yourself a lawyer?

DEB: Not yet.

PETER: They're bloody expensive.

DEB: I don't know where we're gonna find one we can afford.

TRISH: I can help.

Everyone turns to look at TRISH. *Beat.*

KENNETH: D'you know someone, Trish?

TRISH: Me.

KENNETH: Come again?

TRISH: I'm a solicitor, Ken.

KENNETH: Thought you were training with Deb to get your commercial licence?

TRISH: I am.

KENNETH: So you're a lawyer *and* a pilot?

DEB: I didn't think to ask—I know how busy you are.

TRISH: Not anymore. Told the boss I was expecting and he sacked me.

KENNETH: *And* pregnant.

TRISH: There's only so many matinee jackets you can sew before you want to top yourself.

KENNETH: That's a bit dark.

DEB: Well, I wouldn't want to feel responsible for your demise, Trish.

TRISH: Great.

DEB *starts to take off* RICHARD*'s clothes.*

And I dare say no-one at Ansett will be bilingual.

KENNETH: Come again?

TRISH: I speak aviation *and* law.

RICHARD: I gotta hit the road. Wanna lift Ken?

KENNETH: Yep. Night all.

They all say their goodnights. RICHARD *and* KENNETH *exit.*

PETER: Full disclosure, Trish, now Deb's quit the high school—

TRISH: You quit?

DEB: I want Ansett to know I'm serious.

TRISH: Smart move.

PETER: —now she's quit we don't have a heap of money but maybe / she could—

TRISH: Don't be stupid, I'll do it for free.

PETER / DEB: Really?

TRISH: Course. If Deb wins this we'll be making history.

Beat.

You'll need a great barrister though.

PETER: Got any ideas?

TRISH: I do, actually.

SKINNY BLOKES THAT FLY. OFFICE OF JOHN DWYER. 1978.

DEB *and* PETER *sit in the incredibly chaotic office of* JOHN DWYER*—forties, mad-professor type.* TRISH *moves around, surreptitiously trying to tidy some of the mess.*

In DEB*'s eyeline, through the window, is a bright orange billboard with the word 'ANSETT' emblazoned across it.*

DWYER *holds court.*

DWYER: I'm surrounded by strong women, you see, so the idea of women having careers is not an anathema to me. My wife's a lawyer. Mother-in-law's a doctor. I'm well aware of the barriers that stand in the way of women and their work. For, '*Injustice anywhere is a threat to justice everywhere.*'

Beat.

DEB: So you'll take my case, Mr Dwyer?

DWYER: I certainly will. And call me John. If this new anti-discrimination law has teeth, it will be a beacon for all who know that true equality is the only way forward. I believe we can argue it, I believe we can defend it, I believe we can win it.

Beat. He reaches for a set of papers.

Having said that—Ansett's asked to be exempt from it.

DEB: *Exempt* from what?

TRISH: *The Equal Opportunity Act*.

DEB: Can they do that?

DWYER: They can *ask*.

PETER: We haven't even got to court / yet!

DEB: On what grounds?

DWYER: They're saying airlines '*shouldn't have to adhere to the same laws as other businesses*' because they have different '*safety concerns*.'

TRISH: In order to '*meet*' those safety concerns, Ansett believes they need an '*all-male*' crew.

DEB: Because men are safer?

DWYER: More—'*Frailty thy name is / woman.*'

TRISH: They claim you won't have the '*strength*' to handle the bigger aircraft.

DEB: That's crap—you don't need a lot of strength.

PETER: Have you seen some of the skinny blokes that / fly commercial?

TRISH: / Oh, I know.

DWYER: Which is why Fay suggested that if they truly believe that, they should apply for the exemption.

Beat. PETER *and* DEB *look at each other.*

PETER: I thought Fay was on our side.

TRISH: She is.

PETER: Then why's she advising *them* on how they can be *exempt*?

TRISH *moves a mountain of paper to get to a stapled set of papers under it.*

DWYER: Don't move them.

TRISH: Really?

DWYER: '*Though this be madness, yet there is method in't.*'

TRISH *puts the papers back,* DWYER *expertly grabs the ones she's looking for, hands them to her.* TRISH *flicks though them then hands it to* DEB.

TRISH: After speaking with Sir Reg during the conciliation process, Fay knew that strength was going to come up as an argument in court. So she collected a whole lot of data from international airlines where female pilots were employed and … Page four, Deb.

DEB *flicks to find it.* PETER *reads over her shoulder.*

DWYER: The air safety records of women are actually *superior* to men.

TRISH: Which means Ansett'll have Buckley's of proving their claim.

DWYER: And if they can't *prove* you're unsafe, they can't get an exemption.

DEB: Right.

TRISH: Fay reckons, if Ansett's exemption's refused, their objection to your application'll probably be withdrawn.

A sudden thought occurs to PETER, *who jumps up.*

PETER: That definitely makes the offer bullshit!

TRISH: What offer?

PETER: Show 'em the letter, Deb.

DWYER: What's this?

DEB *grabs a letter from her bag and hands it to* TRISH.

DEB: Came in the post yesterday, from Ansett, inviting me to '*reapply*' for the trainee programme.

PETER: Which was suss, because in the rejection letter they said '*don't bother applying again*'.

DWYER: That's an interesting play.

TRISH *reads from the Ansett letter.*

TRISH: They're suggesting this time she'll be dealt with in accordance with '*the provisions of the Equal Opportunity Act*'.

DEB: So *yesterday* they said I should apply again with the promise they'll *follow* the law, and *today* they want to be *exempt* from it?

PETER: Bastards.

DWYER *reads from the exemption request papers.*

DWYER: Three years?

Beat.

TRISH: More context, John?

DWYER: Ansett's applying for the exemption ' ... *for a period of three years*'. Why's that?

TRISH: You can't be accepted into the training programme once you turn twenty-seven.

DEB: In three years I'll be too old.

DWYER *is almost impressed by their tactics.*

DWYER: '*To look like th' innocent flower, but be the serpent under 't.*'

TRISH: I'm gonna make a copy of Ansett's offer.

TRISH *exits with Deb's Ansett offer. Beat.* DEB *points out the window.*

DEB: Is that bothering anyone else?

DWYER *speaks without looking up.*

DWYER: What's that?

DEB: The giant orange Ansett ad plastered on the side of that building.

DWYER *looks up.*

DWYER: Never noticed it before.

DEB: I can't help thinking it's a sign.

DWYER: It's definitely a sign.

THE WORLD'S CHANGING. JANUARY 1979.

REG ANSETT *and* FRANK PASCOE *stand in an office.*

REG: You said all this would be over once I talked to that mad woman from Equal Opportunity Office.

FRANK: I thought it would be.

REG: But it's not over, is it, Frank?

FRANK: No, sir.

REG: Was I not clear, Frank?

FRANK: You were clear, sir. There will be no women on any of your flight decks under any circumstances.

REG: That's right, Frank.

FRANK: I mean, our surveys have shown passengers prefer to fly with a fatherly figure.

REG: Exactly. So how did this girl get past the gate?

FRANK: From what I understand, Theunissen was only getting her in to strike her off the list.

REG: But he didn't strike her off, did he, Frank?

FRANK: No, sir. From what I can understand the Captains were so impressed with her they had no choice but to give her a psych test.

REG: There's always a choice, Frank.

FRANK: And from what I understand, once she rated well in *that,* they wanted to offer her a trainee position. But I made it very clear, Reg, that was never going to happen on my watch. And we sent her a rejection letter.

REG: Then why are we having this conversation, Frank?

FRANK: She rejected it.

REG: She rejected the rejection letter?

FRANK: Yes, sir.

REG: How's that possible?

FRANK: It's these new laws, / Reg!

REG: I built this company from nothing, Frank.

FRANK: I know, / Reg.

REG: No-one has the right to tell me how to run it.

FRANK: I know.

Beat.

It's just … It seems like the world's changing.

Beat.

REG: Not at Ansett, it isn't.

INTERVAL

ACT TWO

PAMELA REPORTS 1. AN HISTORIC DAY. 1979.

PAMELA GRAHAM, *movie-star looks, great hair, stands out the front of the Equal Opportunity Board, microphone in hand.* TED*—her cameraman—films her.*

PAMELA: Pamela Graham reporting on an historic day here in Victoria, where the newly appointed Equal Opportunity Board is hearing its first ever case. A twenty-five year old woman by the name of Deborah Lawrie has accused Ansett Airlines of discrimination for failing to employ her in their July trainee pilot intake. Stay tuned as I bring you all the breaking news during this watershed case.

1ST EOB HEARING. DAY ONE. 1979.

A nervous but hopeful DEB *sits at the EOB, eyes glued on* DWYER *as he questions* GARTH HARRIS [DEB*'s flying instructor*].

DWYER: Mr Harris, you taught Deborah Lawrie to fly; if you could cast your mind back, how did you rate Miss Lawrie?

GARTH: She was a star pupil.

DWYER: Would you be so kind as to elaborate?

GARTH: Deb was very focussed and she was a very quick learner. She was only sixteen when she first flew solo.

DWYER: Sixteen?

GARTH: And she did it after only eleven hours.

DWYER: That's good, is it?

GARTH: Well, it usually takes a student an average of fifteen. And Deb could only afford one lesson a month, / so—

DWYER: So she had eleven one-hour lessons, over eleven months?

GARTH: That's right. And that meant between lessons she had to remember everything she'd learnt and practise using only her imagination. It takes a certain kind of discipline to do that.

DWYER: Did anything else make Miss Lawrie stand out?

GARTH: When Deb got her *instrument* rating—

DWYER: Which / is?

GARTH: The rating you get flying *solely* by reference to instruments. She scored very, very highly.

DWYER: What do you think contributed to that high score?

GARTH: Deb has a very clear mind. Her manipulative skill is excellent. And the aircraft she got her rating on, the Twin Comanche, is one of the most difficult planes to fly coz it doesn't have contra-rotating props.

DWYER: Props?

GARTH: Propellers. They both turn the *same* way. Making it much more difficult to handle if you … say, lose an engine.

DWYER: I see.

GARTH: Deb rated the *highest* of any person I've ever trained.

DWYER: Any *woman*?

GARTH: No, any person.

DEB *smiles shyly and looks down.*

DWYER: So, in your opinion, Deborah Lawrie is unusually gifted, highly dedicated, and supremely skilled?

GARTH: Yes.

DWYER: Hmmm.

Beat.

If only she were born a man.

DEB *looks to* DWYER, *impressed.*

HOSTIES. YOU'RE A VERY PRETTY GIRL. PLANE ENTRANCE. 1979.

GLENDA *and* PATRICIA *stand at the plane's entrance waiting to welcome the passengers.*

PATRICIA: I'm dying for an update.

GLENDA: An update on what?

FIRST OFFICER BRUCE WOODRIDGE, *carry-bag in hand, enters the plane.*

PATRICIA: / Morning, Bruce.

GLENDA: / Good morning, First Officer Woodbridge.

GLENDA *takes his bag and* BRUCE *heads off.*

PATRICIA: Fly Girl has her hearing today and I'm stuck on a double.

GLENDA: Mr Hayden says it's all just a case of sour grapes.

PATRICIA: Does he now?

GLENDA: He says it's not ethical to hire people who aren't up to scratch just because they have a tantrum. And Patricia, I'm inclined to agree. I mean, I'm sorry she's disappointed but I don't think she should be advertising it to all and sundry. Plus, I don't think it's fair that Reg is being *forced* to hire her.

PATRICIA: The only thing Reg is being forced to do, is consider her in the same way he considers the men who apply. That's it, Glenda. Nothing more, nothing less.

GLENDA: Huh ... Well, Pat, I'm not sure how I feel about that until I talk to Hayden. Till then, I guess we'll have to agree to disagree.

MARGARET *enters, straightening her uniform to begin her shift.*

MARGARET: Fly Girl's case just broke for lunch.

PATRICIA: What's happened, Marg?

MARGARET *fills the drinks trolley and* PATRICIA *helps in between welcoming guests.*

MARGARET: This morning, Fly Girl's team had their go and apparently they were very convincing. But get this—

MR KING *arrives with a suit bag.*

GLENDA: Hello, Mr King, can I grab that for you?

MR KING *hands over his suit bag and stands a bit too close.*

MR KING: Thank you, darling. Brenda, isn't it?

GLENDA: Glenda, / actually.

MARGARET: I'll take that, Glenda.

MARGARET *grabs the suit bag and goes to put it away.*

MR KING: You're a very pretty girl, a very good girl, Brenda.

PATRICIA / MARGARET: Glenda.

GLENDA: / Glenda. Just doing my job, Mr King.

MR KING: I look forward to you taking care of me today, sweetheart.

MR KING *rests his hand on* GLENDA*'s lower back and she steps slightly to the left and out.* MARGARET *and* PATRICIA *make eyes at each other.*

PATRICIA: Actually, Mr King, I'm up the front today.

GLENDA: Are you?

PATRICIA: Remember …

MR KING: Oh.

MR KING *is disappointed.*

Next time.

PATRICIA *fakes a smile.* MR KING *heads off.*

GLENDA: Thanks, Pat.

PATRICIA: Don't mention it. Go on, Marg.

MARGARET: Fly Girl's mum's friend works at the place they do the psych testing—

PATRICIA: You're joking?

MARGARET: And Fly Girl's mum's friend told Fly Girl she came top three out of all the candidates!

PATRICIA: You're joking?

MARGARET: But then the Ansett lawyer presented a *signed affidavit* from Fly Girl's mum's friend saying that conversation … never happened!

GLENDA: So Fly Girl's lying?

PATRICIA: Well, someone is.

1ST EOB RULING. DEIDRE FITZGERALD. 1979.

DEB *sits in a spotlight and listens to* CHAIRWOMAN DEIDRE FITZGERALD *deliver her ruling.*

DEIDRE: Quieten down, thank you. The Board has considered the matter, and finds that the respondent Ansett Transport Industries has unlawfully discriminated against the complainant Deborah Lawrie in failing to accept her as a trainee pilot in the July 1978 intake.

DEB *looks hopeful.*

The Board orders the respondent to refrain from committing any further act of discrimination against the complainant, and further orders that she be the first person admitted to the next intake of trainee pilots by the respondent company.

DEB *is elated. Noises fill the courtroom. These slowly turn to objections. We hear the voices of* ANSETT LAWYERS.

ANSETT LAWYER 1: This is ridiculous! We're here to ascertain whether there is a case to answer to. Not for you to hand down orders.

ANSETT LAWYER 2: Bunch of amateurs. This is procedural / ineptitude.

ANSETT LAWYER 3: Procedural ineptitude. You have prejudged the case!

DEIDRE: Quieten down, quieten down, please. We the Board hear your concerns and hereby withdraw the statement and rescind our orders. We will take a short recess and reconvene soon.

1ST EOB HEARING. PROCEDURAL INEPTITUDE. DAY ONE. 1979.

DEB, PETER, DWYER *and* TRISH *walk hurriedly along a corridor to a lift.*

PETER: Why the hell did the Board go back on their decision?!

DWYER: They shouldn't have handed down those orders.

DEB: That's why we're here, isn't it?!

They all stop at the lift. DWYER *hits the down button.*

DWYER: The Board's here to decide whether you *have a case to answer*.

DEB: So I don't start training in July?!

DWYER: Deidre Fitzgerald jumped the gun when she made the orders.

TRISH: Which is why she revoked them.

DEB:Is this a joke?

DWYER: Yours is the first case to be contested under the Equal Opportunity Act. Bound to be teething problems.

The lift doors open and they all move inside. DWYER hits the ground button. Doors close. DEB turns to PETER.

DEB: And how could Mary say that conversation never / happened?

TRISH: Don't worry, Deb.

DWYER: Don't fret, Deborah.

DEB: I'm gonna call her / and—

TRISH: / You can't!

DWYER: Absolutely not!

TRISH: You got to keep your trap shut, Deb! John's subpoenaed your Chandler Macleod results.

DWYER: So next time we're in court, we'll have the evidence to support your claim.

Ding. The doors open and they all step out and into a throng of reporters and camera flashes.

PETER: We're coming back?!

DWYER: We have to *prove* there's *a case to answer to.*

DEB: We *won* the case and now we have to prove there *is* one? What a waste of time.

DWYER: You call it a waste of time, we call it the legal process.

DEB CALLS MARY PERRETT. 1979. NIGHT.

We hear the ringing of a phone. Spot up on a nervous DEB. *A spot up on a worried-looking* MARY PERRETT. *She watches the phone ring. Beat. She picks it up.*

MARY: Perrett residence?

DEB: Mary?! Don't hang up.

MARY: You shouldn't be / calling.

DEB: Why did you lie?

MARY: I can't go into / it.

DEB: If you hadn't told me how well I'd done, I wouldn't have gone to the Board in the first place.

MARY: I told you that in / confidence.

DEB: You signed an affidavit that wasn't true!

MARY: They were going to take my job!

Beat.

DEB: Who? … Who, Mary? … Ansett?

Beat.

MARY: Don't call again.

MARY *hangs up.*

PAMELA REPORTS 2. 1ST EOB HEARING. DAY TWO. 1979.

PAMELA *reports. Cameraman* TED *films. Two other reporters,* REPORTER 1 *and* REPORTER 2 *stand nearby, awaiting the arrival of* DEB *and her legal team.*

PAMELA: Day two of the Deborah Lawrie discrimination case and Ansett argues the EOB *prejudged* the matter in favour of Miss Lawrie. After hours of legal back-and-forth, a resolution looks unlikely as Ansett attempts to / have the Board—

DEB *exits the building and into a flurry of noise and camera flashes.* REPORTER 1 *and* REPORTER 2 *thrust microphones in her face.* DEB *tries to escape the throng.*

REPORTER 1: Miss Lawrie, / Miss Lawrie.

REPORTER 2: Were you surprised at today's proceedings?

DEB: I had no idea Ansett could ask the Board to *disqualify* itself.

REPORTER 1: Do *you* believe the Board *prejudged* your case?

DEB: [*fobbing them off*] I don't think so, I don't know! I have to meet my fiancé at the car—

DEB *tries to leave. They block her.*

REPORTER 2: So you'll / be back in court again?

DEB: I have to find my fiancé!

PAMELA: Stop the camera, Ted.

TED *lowers his camera.* PAMELA *walks towards* DEB. DEB *tries to move again but is blocked.*

REPORTER 1: / Just a minute of your time, Miss Lawrie, do you—

REPORTER 2: Just one more question! How is it—

PAMELA: How about you guys just step back! Step back!

The REPORTERS *move off to chase Ansett's legal team.*

REPORTER 1: Mr Haynes, can you / explain why you believe the Board prejudged the case?

REPORTER 2: Mr Haynes, a moment of your time!

The two women are left alone. PAMELA *looks at* DEB *fondly, weighing up whether she should speak.*

PAMELA: Pamela Graham, journalist.

DEB: Deb.

Beat.

PAMELA: It's a hell of a lot.

DEB: Hell of a lot.

Beat.

It's so unfair.

PAMELA: I've covered a lot of cases, they're never fair.

DEB: I'm starting to realise that.

PAMELA: Ansett's a big corporation with millions of dollars behind them. More money means more man power to work out all the ways they can use the law to stop you getting what you want.

DEB: Good to know.

PAMELA: But you have one thing they don't.

DEB: What's that?

PAMELA: You're likeable.

Beat.

This won't just be lost or won in the courtroom, Deborah. If enough people get behind you, it really could swing this case.

DEB: You think so?

PAMELA: I do.

Beat.

There's no doubt the media are a pack of vultures. But they're vultures you want on your side. You can't control what they say in the court room. But every day, after it's over, you *can* come out here to tell *your* side of the story.

DEB: Every day?! How long do you think it'll take?

PAMELA: I'd prepare for a marathon if I were you.

DEB: A marathon? I'm getting married in nine days.

THREE-TIER WEDDING CAKE. DEB'S HOUSE. 1979.

Empty lounge room. A phone starts to ring and continues throughout the scene.

PETER: [*off*] Deb? Deb? Deeeeb?! Can you answer that?
DEB: [*off*] I'm getting dressed for court, Pete. I've gotta leave in five.

PETER, *dressed in an apron, holding a spatula and an icing piping bag enters the lounge room.*

PETER: DL, I can't pick it up, my hands are sticky. I've gotta get this icing on before it hardens. If I don't finish it now, it won't be set for our wedding.

He exits.

DEB: [*off*] Bugger.

DEB *enters in a terry towelling robe, hair wrapped in a towel.*

[*Shouting off*] I can't keep wearing the same thing, Pete. It's embarrassing. The press keep taking photos—it looks like I don't have any other clothes.

PETER: [*off*] Ansett wear the same thing every day.

DEB: [*shouting off*] They're men, Peter. No-one cares what they look like.

DEB *takes a breath and picks up the phone.*

DEB: Deborah Lawrie speaking. Yes, yes, I've got a minute. Of course I'm frustrated. Yes, I must admit I'm finding the whole legal process pretty tedious—

The door bell rings.

DEB: Hang on a tick.

DEB *covers the phone and shouts.*

Peter, the / door!

PETER: [*off*] I can't move DL, I'm attaching the third tier—

DEB: [*shouting off*] The Age is on / the phone.

PETER: [*off*] I can't let go until the icing has hardened to the pillars. If I do, the whole thing could come down and there goes cutting / our wedding cake.

The door bell rings again, and urgent knocking.

DEB: [*back to the phone*] Sorry, I'm gonna have to get the door. Yep. Bye.

DEB *hangs up. The phone starts up again.*

DEB: Bloody hell.

PETER: [*off*] Just leave it, Deb. They'll call back.

DEB *exits. A beat later,* MUM *and* TRISH*'s voices can be heard.*

DEB: [*off*] Why are you here, Mum? I'm not trying on the dress again!

The phone stops. DEB *rushes back in to the lounge.* MUM *and a more pregnant* TRISH *hustle into the lounge room.* TRISH *is carrying a wedding dress.*

MUM: Wake up, Debbie. The wedding's tomorrow. Trish can't be expected to finish it without a final fitting.

DEB: You can't be here Mum, we've gotta get to court and I don't even know what I'm wearing.

MUM: I told you to buy that extra blouse.

DEB: Oh, thanks / Mum.

MUM: And Trish's driving you to court anyway, so two birds one stone.

TRISH *holds the dress open for* DEB *to step into. Just as the phone starts up again.*

TRISH: Hop in and I'll just quickly pin it.

DEB *steps into the dress as* MUM *goes to answer the phone.*

DEB: Leave it, Mum.

MUM: Have you lost more weight?

TRISH: Everyone does for their / wedding, Dorothy.

The phone stops.

DEB: I'm not trying to, I'm stressed. The press has gone next level. They're taking the worst photos, misquoting what I say. / I sound like an idiot.

MUM: Well, you're gonna look like a skeleton at your wedding.

The phone starts up again.

DEB: Thanks Mum, can't do much about / that now.

PETER: [*off*] Do you need me to grab that?

DEB: Don't come in!!
MUM: No! Don't come in!!
TRISH: It's bad luck! [*To* DEB] You can step out.

DEB *gets out of the dress and rushes off.*

DEB: I gotta get ready.
TRISH: [*shouting to* DEB] I'm gonna have to take it in a bit, Deb. Can I come over in the morning?
PETER: [*off*] Can I come in now?
MUM / TRISH: Yes!

PETER *enters sans apron and picks up the phone.*

PETER: Peter Wardley speaking. That's right, big day tomorrow. In fact I've just been putting the final touches on our wedding cake. Yep, Deb and I are prepared to go right to the end. Even if it means going bankrupt. No, no, I'm just the man-behind-the-woman—confronting-the-other-man … men.

He hangs up.

MUM: [*shouting off*] Well, I'll get going, Debbie. Just wear that lovely plaid skirt I got you from Georges. That'll send the right message. Trish has gotta do the last-minute adjustments *on you*, Debbie. Nine a.m. work?
DEB: [*off*] I won't be here.
PETER: She won't be here.
TRISH: / Where will you be?
MUM: [*shouting off*] Where will you be? [*Back to* PETER] Where will she be?
DEB: [*off*] It's the Freda Thompson Air Race—
TRISH / PETER: Round Port Phillip Bay.
MUM: [*shouting off*] No, Deborah, it's your wedding day.
TRISH: [*shouting off*] I'll be in the car, Deb.

TRISH *exits with wedding dress.* DEB *re-enters.*

DEB: Mum, it's the most important event in the racing calendar.
MUM: Can't you give it a miss?
DEB: I'd just spend all day thinking about it.
MUM: What do you think about this, Peter?
PETER: She is who she is.

DEB: I'm determined to win it this year, Mum. It'll be too stressful if I miss it.
MUM: It'll be too stressful if you miss your wedding.
PETER: You're definitely coming to the wedding though, right, DL?
DEB: Wouldn't miss it for the world.

DEB *kisses* PETER *and exits.*

PAMELA REPORTS 3. INJUNCTION DAY. 1979.

A charged-up PAMELA *reports:*

PAMELA: Miss Lawrie returned to the Equal Opportunity Board today with hopes her discrimination case would be over *before* her wedding tomorrow. This will not to be the case, however, as Ansett has served the Board with an injunction from the Supreme Court, halting proceedings until further notice.

DWYER *exits the court.*

Mr Dwyer, can I have your thoughts on today's events?
DWYER: It would appear that, armed with the sinews of war, the respondent intends to continue this protracted campaign which has already placed tremendous stress, both personal and financial, on my client.

PAMELA REPORTS 4. IT'S RATHER FRUSTRATING. SUPREME COURT. 1979.

TED *films* PAMELA *at the front of the Supreme Court. A fuming* DEB *stands to the side.*

PAMELA: This morning, the newly married Deborah Wardley took to the Supreme Court. After mounting pressure from Ansett's new QC Peter Liddell, Supreme Court Justice Beach said he needed more time to consider the matter; restraining the EOB from hearing the case until further notice. Mrs Wardley...

PAMELA *notices* DEB*'s mood.*

Hold the roll Ted. Do you need a moment, Deb?
DEB: Yeah.

DEB *takes some deep breaths and tries to settle herself. Beat.*

PAMELA: I know I'm s'posed to remain impartial but that Liddell is a complete prick—

TED: [*sotto*] Pammy.

PAMELA / DEB: He is.

PAMELA: [*to* TED] He's revelling in trying to destroy her character. [*To* DEB] Well done for managing to keep calm in there.

DEB: I'm so pissed off.

PAMELA: Of course. But there's nothing the Australian public likes less than an angry woman. So just get it all out before we roll up.

Beat.

Turn around, Ted.

PAMELA *and TED turn their back on* DEB *and she lets fly.*

DEB: Shitfuckshitfuckshitfuckshit! Fuck that fucker. Fuuuuuuck.

PAMELA: [*smiling*] Better?

DEB *nods, takes a breath and goes into a 'TV mode' we've never seen before.*

PAMELA *looks into the camera, now completely professional.*

Mrs Wardley, how does it feel to have this halt in proceedings with no indication as to when your case will recommence.

DEB: Well … it's rather frustrating.

PAMELA: I can imagine. QC Liddell claims that by forcing Ansett to hire you the EOB has '*no regard for public safety*'. What's your opinion on that?

DEB: Mr Liddell is doing his best to humiliate and discredit me but obviously he's just saying whatever Mr Ansett wants him to say.

PAMELA: Have you met Mr Ansett?

DEB: He's nowhere to be seen.

PAMELA: Now the case has been suspended do you think you'll stop fighting?

DEB: Mr Ansett can try whatever tactics he likes but I plan to fight this to the very end.

HOSTIES. CHICKEN OR BEEF 1. PLANE AISLE. 1979.

Lights up on MARGARET *and* GLENDA *in the aisle together serving unseen customers.*

GLENDA / MARGARET: [*to customer*] / The chicken or the beef?
MARGARET: Did you see, after *a month* of dilly-dallying, Dick Hamer's finally / appointed—
GLENDA: Dick who?
MARGARET: The premier, Glenda. He's finally appointed a *new* Board to hear Fly Girl's case. [*To customer*] The chicken or the beef?
GLENDA: So she has to start this thing all over again?
MARGARET: Yep. [*To customer*] The chicken or the beef?
GLENDA: Has she had her honeymoon yet?!
MARGARET: They keep dragging her back to court, Glen, so there's no time for a honeymoon
GLENDA: Well that's a bad omen. [*To customer*] / The chicken or the beef?
MARGARET: The chicken or the beef?

2ND EOB HEARING. DON'T ELABORATE. 1979.

DEB, PETER *and* TRISH *move into the elevator at the EOB.* PETER *presses the button.*

TRISH: Don't be thrown, Ansett's got a new Head of Counsel.
DEB: Another one?
TRISH: Don Ryan. Plus there's a few extra lawyers hanging 'round.
DEB: At least Liddell's / gone!

A dishevelled DWYER *rushes in.*

TRISH: Remember, when you're on the stand, answer down the line.
DWYER: '*It is not enough to speak, but to speak true.*'
DEB: Got / it.
DWYER: And '*brevity is the soul of wit*'. So …
TRISH: Don't run your mouth off.

Lift door opens, they alight.

THE 2ND EOB HEARING. 1979.

DEB *is on the stand. She is being questioned by* QC DON RYAN.

RYAN: Mrs Wardley, I'd like you to cast your mind back to a *small* charter company operating out of Essendon airport. Did you apply for a job as a pilot with this company?

DEB: I did.

RYAN: Yet it would seem you were never employed by this company, were you?

DEB: … No I wasn't.

RYAN: I imagine with a *small* charter company the competition wouldn't have been too fierce, would it?

DEB: I suppose not.

RYAN: So in that particular case you were rejected because you simply weren't good enough. Just as you were rejected at Ansett, Mrs Wardley, because you simply weren't good enough.

DEB: I wasn't rejected, I withdrew my application.

RYAN: … Withdrew it?

RYAN *is confused by this information and starts shuffling papers.*

And w … why would you do that?

DEB: I found out the company's aircraft maintenance wasn't up to scratch. And I didn't want to work for a company that … wasn't safe.

Chuckles and hubbub throughout the courtroom.

PAMELA REPORTS 5. PREGNANCY AND MOTHERHOOD. 1979.

PAMELA: Yesterday, Ansett were concerned Mrs Wardley's '*earrings*' getting '*caught on her headphones*' could be '*a safety factor.*' Today, the Ansett camp's claiming it's not '*safety*' but '*pregnancy and motherhood*' standing in the way of hiring newly married Deborah Wardley. Members of Ansett's management team will take the stand this afternoon.

2ND EOB HEARING. DWYER QUESTIONS ANSETT MANAGEMENT. 1979.

ANSETT MANAGEMENT *speak on the stand.* DEB *watches on.*

MR TYLER MOORE: You can't possibly be a dedicated mother and a dedicated pilot at the same time. It's better to focus on one thing.

Lights down. Lights up.

MR ARTHUR: My wife's role is in the home and I think that's the appropriate place for a woman to be.

Beat.

And that women are happier there.

Lights down. Lights up.

MR WHITE: Pregnancy, is it a disease?

HOSTIES. IS PREGNANCY A DISEASE? THE GALLEY. 1979.

PATRICIA, GLENDA *and* MARGARET *stand reading the paper in the galley. The front headline reads, 'PREGNANCY, IS IT A DISEASE?'*

PATRICIA: They're changing arguments like hats on bloody race day.

GLENDA: Women *do* get sick when they've got a bun in the oven, Pat. My cousin Christine couldn't keep a thing down when she was pregnant / with Christopher.

PATRICIA: Not everyone's your cousin / Christine.

CAPTAIN BRUCE: [*voiceover*] Cabin crew, arm the slides and prepare the cabin for takeoff.

GLENDA *and* MARGARET *do their cross check.*

GLENDA: But they have a point about the dizzy spells, don't they?

MARGARET: There's always two pilots in the cockpit, Glenda.

PATRICIA: Besides, there's as much chance of your pregnant co-pilot passing out from being *dizzy* as there is of your male co-pilot having a heart attack.

MARGARET: All the men in my life have died from heart attacks.

GLENDA: / Ooh, don't say that.

GLENDA *makes the sign of the cross.*

PATRICIA: Exactly. No-one thinks of *that* when they go up in a plane.

GLENDA, MARGARET *and* PATRICIA *sit down and buckle up.*

GLENDA: But girls, ladies *are* different you know, because of our cycles. We're moody, aren't we?

PATRICIA: Fly Girl's gyno said she doesn't get / moody.

MARGARET: She's never even had PMS.

PATRICIA: Done some of her hardest flying on her period.

GLENDA: How do you know all this?

MARGARET: They've been talking about it all week in court.

GLENDA: How embarrassing.

PATRICIA: What's embarrassing, Glenda, is that Ansett just makes up bullshit so they don't have to give Fly Girl a job and when someone calls them out on it, they make up more.

2ND EOB HEARING. PUT YOUR HAND UP. 1979.

DWYER *and* DEB *enter the EOB to take their seats.* DWYER *motions to the gallery and speaks in a hushed tone.*

DWYER: The Captains present at your interview are giving evidence today.

DEB *looks over and gives a nod and a smile.*

DEB: Well, I was sent to the Chandler Macleod psych appraisal so maybe it won't be too bad.

DWYER: Even so, if there's anything they say on the stand you know to be untrue, just put your hand up so Trish can see it, and I'll deal with it my end.

2ND EOB HEARING. THREE OR FOUR. 1979.

The ANSETT LAWYER interviews the uneasy CAPTAINS.

RYAN: Captain Ball, did Mrs Wardley mention if she was thinking of having any children?

CAPTAIN BALL: I believe it was three or four.

DEB *gives a small raise of her hand.* TRISH *gestures to* DWYER.

Lights down. Lights up.

RYAN: And do you recall, Captain Burnett, how many children Mrs Wardley said she she'd like?

CAPTAIN BURNETT: Three or four.

DEB *raises her hand again.* TRISH *gives the nod to* DWYER.

Lights down. Lights up.

RYAN: Captain Tomlin, how many children did Mrs Wardley say she was planning on having?

CAPTAIN TOMLIN: Yes. I remember one of the Captains asking her and she said she'd love to have '*three or four*'.

DEB *raises her hand again.*

DWYER: I ask the Board that the Ansett Captains be removed from the room so we may ascertain whether their recollections are entirely their own.

HOSTIES DEBRIEF ON THE PLANE 1. THE GALLEY. 1979.

GLENDA *and* PATRICIA *prepare the trolleys.*

PATRICIA: And when Dwyer kicked them out they couldn't corroborate their lies anymore so none of their stories added up.

GLENDA: Who knows who was lying?

PATRICIA: Everyone, Glen. Dwyer subpoenaed the notes from Fly Girl's interview and the next time they were in court the truth came out. She actually said she wanted '*Two kids max*'.

GLENDA: Maybe they remembered it wrong.

PATRICIA: Yes, Glenda, they all just happened to remember with absolute certainty something she never said.

Beat.

It's blindingly obvious it doesn't matter how good Fly Girl is—Reg is never gonna let her in.

MARGARET *enters with a trolley to restock.*

MARGARET: Oh Pat, I've been meaning to ask, what ever happened with that divorcee you met?

PATRICIA: Jules? … She's invited me over to watch that new 'women in prison' / show.

MARGARET: *Prisoner*. / That looks good.
PATRICIA: This Friday night.
MARGARET: Oooooh.

GLENDA *arrives.*

GLENDA: What's all this?
MARGARET: Pat met a woman at a protest for Fly Girl.
GLENDA: Protest?! Be careful Pat! You're going to get yourself killed.
PATRICIA: Don't be / ridiculous..
GLENDA: My Hayden says that protests are for hippies and reprobates. And the cops use all sorts of deterrents nowadays. Tear gas, rubber bullets. They can drag you into a paddy wagon by your hair.
PATRICIA: It's not bloody Vietnam, Glen.
GLENDA: Not trying to be a downer girls but what difference can a whole lot of ladies at a rally really make?
PATRICIA: Never underestimate the power of the people.

SOMEONE'S NUMBER. DEB AND PETE'S LOUNGE ROOM. 1979.

DEB *enters, having just returned from court to find* PETER *at home. Their conversation is a strained but they are both trying.*

DEB: Why didn't you come to court today?
PETER: Got tied up at work and then it seemed late and—how was it?
DEB: One of the management team admitted he '*might have discriminated against me*' but only '*because I was a woman*'.
PETER: You're joking.
DEB: And that wasn't even the craziest thing that happened.

DEB *reaches into her pocket, pulls out the piece of paper.*

I was leaving court, someone pushed this in to my hand and said, "You need to call this number", then disappeared into thin air.
PETER: Who?
DEB: I dunno. I didn't see them.
PETER: Give it here.

DEB *hands it over.* PETER *reads it.*

Has some bloke given you his number?

DEB: What? / No!

DEB *grabs the paper, moves to the telephone and starts dialling.*

PETER: Oh-eight? That's Perth.

DEB: I don't know anyone from Perth—

PETER: Not a pilot?

DEB: I'm not gonna run off with a pilot, Pete! How many times do I have to / say it?

PETER: What are you doing?

DEB: Calling it.

DEB *holds the phone to her ear. We hear ringing. It's a bit tense. Suddenly a voice answers and lights come up on a teen* GIRL.

GIRL: Hello?

DEB: Hello. Who's this?

GIRL: Who's *this*?

DEB: Someone gave me this number.

GIRL: What? Who?

DEB: I don't know.

GIRL: I'm confused.

DEB: So am I.

GIRL: Can I just … grab your name?

DEB *looks to* PETER.

DEB: Deb Wardley.

GIRL: Deborah Wardley? Crikey Moses! Carol, Carol, Deborah Wardley's on the phone!!

CAROL REINER *runs in and takes the phone from the teen* GIRL.

CAROL REINER: Hello Deborah. I'm Carol Reiner, secretary of the Women's Electoral Lobby in Perth. I'm sorry the way we got in contact was so … clandestine.

DEB: It does feel a bit cloak and dagger.

CAROL REINER: We couldn't risk Ansett cottoning on to what we've got.

DEB: What have you got?

CAROL REINER: I read in the press Ansett offered you the opportunity to *reapply* for their trainee pilot programme? The idea being *this* time, as they assessed you, they'd *comply* with the provisions of the Equal Opportunity Act?

DEB: That's correct.

CAROL REINER: Well we've been corresponding with Ansett for some time now and *yesterday,* we received correspondence from the General Manager that we'd like to gift your legal team.

2ND EOB HEARING. A VERY NICE PERSON. 1979.

DWYER: We'd like to submit a *new* piece of evidence, that's recently come to hand. Oops, wrong glasses.

DWYER *switches his glasses.*

Nope, not this one.

DWYER *puts down the paper and picks up another.*

Bingo. The Women's Electoral Lobby, Perth, sent a letter to Ansett, threatening to *boycott* their airline if they did not hire Mrs Wardley. They received this response from General Manager, Frank Pascoe, just a few days ago. '*Sir Reginald Ansett has asked me to thank you for your letter regarding the application by Mrs Deborah Wardley* (*née Lawrie*) *for employment with our organisation as a pilot. We have a good record of employing females in a wide range of positions within our organisation / but have* adopted a policy of only employing men as pilots.'

Lights up on a stately looking FRANK PASCOE *sits in a stately chair.*

FRANK: … but have *adopted a policy* of *only employing men as pilots*.

DWYER *looks purposefully to the Board.*

This does not mean that women cannot be good pilots, but we are concerned with the provisions of the safest and most efficient service possible. *In this regard we feel that an all-male crew is safer than one in which the sexes are mixed.*

We thank you for your interest in Mrs Wardley's case and I am sure you will be pleased to know that I have met Mrs Wardley and find her a very nice person, highly intelligent and undoubtedly a good pilot, but that is not quite what we are talking about.

We would ask you to reconsider your decision not to patronise our airline. As we feel sure your organisation would not wish / to discriminate against our company—

Lights down on FRANK.

DWYER: ' ... *to discriminate against our company when we are genuinely endeavouring to operate our airline to the highest standard of safety.*'

Beat. DWYER *holds the letter aloft.*

I charge that *this letter* is as plain a statement of *a policy of sexual discrimination* as it would be possible to have.

PAMELA REPORTS 6. ANATOMY SHOULD NOT BE DESTINY. JUNE 6TH. 1979.

A chuffed PAMELA *stands out the front of the EOB, microphone in hand.*

PAMELA: Monumental statements in court today as the Equal Opportunity Board announced that Ansett Transport Industries has discriminated against Deborah Wardley on the grounds of sex. The Board went on to say, '*The childbearing potential of women should not be used to limit women's roles in society.*' A clear declaration for working women across Australia that, '*Anatomy should not be destiny.*'

SPREADING THE WORD 1. JUNE 27TH. 1979.

HELEN *sits at a receptionist desk. An intercom light appears on her phone. She presses to answer it.*

BOSS: [*voiceover*] Helen?

HELEN: Yes, Mr Hacker?

BOSS: [*voiceover*] Call Bob, make sure he's still good for golf this arvo?

HELEN: Not a problem, Mr Hacker.

BOSS: [*voiceover*] Oh, and I've noticed in my schedule you've booked me on a TAA flight for Thursday's trip to Sydney?

HELEN: I couldn't get you on an Ansett flight at the time you wanted, Mr Hacker. And it's important to me that I try to get you what you want. Because that's what I want. I want what you want. We want the same thing.

BOSS: [*voiceover*] You're a top bird, Helen. It's a wonder no-one snapped you up.

HELEN: Thanks, Mr Hacker.

BOSS: [*voiceover*] And now you've missed the boat.

Beat.

Remember to pick up some Iced Vovos for the Cottee's meeting tomorrow. And wear something plunging.

The BOSS *laughs,* HELEN *fake-laughs and then releases the intercom button. The smile drains from her face.*

HELEN *looks around to make sure no-one is listening, picks up her handset and dials.*

Lights up on MARGARET, *in her Ansett uniform putting on the finishing touches of her make-up. She picks up the phone.*

MARGARET: Margaret O'Reilly.

HELEN: Marg, it's me.

MARGARET: Oh Helen darling, how's the world of advertising?

HELEN: Full of shit, Marg.

MARGARET: Did you get the invite for my engagement party?

HELEN: Wouldn't miss it for the world.

MARGARET: Super. So, what's news with you?

HELEN *looks around.*

HELEN: Well Marg, I'm part of a revolution.

MARGARET: Geez, that doesn't sound like you.

HELEN: Now I'm eating again, I've had all sorts of ideas. You know how Ansett appealed Fly Girl's win this morning?

MARGARET: I don't live under a rock, darl. It's all anyone at / work's talking about.

HELEN: Well, the hearing's set for the Supreme Court tomorrow and if Ansett get their way, Fly Girl would have to fight her case again. Again.

MARGARET: No.

HELEN: Yes, Marg. Plus Ansett'd be able to bring in new evidence.

MARGARET: Well, that's criminal. I mean, she won fair and square.

HELEN: Exactly. So I got a call from Tall Jenny, who's now working in the city for a big international finance firm. She's in charge of twenty-two girls in the reception team and she's directed them all to stop booking any of their bosses or clients on *any Ansett flights.* Until further notice. She said all the girls in the city law firms are doing the same thing. And now us ladies at the ad firms are on the bandwagon. It's a Girlcott.

MARGARET: A girl what?

HELEN: It's like a boycott run by girls and it's spreading like wildfire, Marg. So pass it on. TAA all the way! Until they let Fly Girl fly!

THE BIGGER THE BETTER. TOWN HALL MEETING. 1979.

CAROLYN KINGHAM *stands on a stage, microphone in hand, next to* DEB. *We hear the sound of a small crowd cheering, chanting, calling out intermittently. i.e. 'Give her a go!' and 'Let her fly!'*

CAROLYN: Settle down everybody, settle down. I'm Carolyn Kingham and I want to thank all of you for being here. I guess everyone's heard the good news. Ansett has *lost* the *first* grounds of their appeal. Which means they have to include Deb in their November trainee intake. How does it feel, Deb?

DEB: I guess you could say we just won round two.

The crowd cheers and whistles.

CAROLYN: And you've got round three to fight in the High Court, later this year!

The crowd boos.

But everyone, this movement we've created, this Girlcott, is having a big impact. Ansett's popularity's waning, which is affecting their bottom line. And that's why it's very important we keep those contributions coming for the *Deb Wardley Fighting Fund*—so Deb can take this all the way!

The crowd goes wild.

How does it feel to have so many supporters, Deb?

DEB: To be honest, it's pretty overwhelming. I'm just very grateful to you and everyone who has turned up today and given money. I never expected this to be such a fuss, but, well here we are.

The crowd laughs and claps.

CAROLYN: Have you got a sense of how this whole thing's going to play out, Deb?

DEB: Well I feel that, whatever the Board decides, it is quite unlikely that I'll ever have a job flying with Ansett. I have a feeling that they're against women.

The crowd boos.

But I am firmly resolved to fight this battle to the end. I think I'm as good a pilot as most men, certainly better than some. But this is not a fight to prove Ansett wrong, I just want to fly jets—the bigger the better.

The crowd cheers.

CAROLYN: If anyone can win this battle, Deb, it's you.

DEB: Well, I'm not going to let one man stand in my way. That's for sure.

SPREADING THE WORD 2. D-DAY GIRLCOTT. JUNE 29TH. 1979.

MARGARET *is on the phone to a riled-up* PATRICIA, *who is surrounded by newly painted protest signs. She holds a paintbrush in her hand.*

MARGARET: What's news, Pat?

PATRICIA: I'm painting placards for the protest.

MARGARET: Beaut, what do they say?

PATRICIA: *Sex before Skill! Who'd Chancett with Mancett*? That sort of thing.

MARGARET: Wish I wasn't rostered on. To be honest, when she won that last appeal I thought that was it! I don't quite understand what the '*second grounds of the appeal*' business even is.

PATRICIA: My Jules has schooled me on this. When Fly Girl finally starts training with Ansett, she'll have to join the pilot's union, right?

MARGARET: Right.

PATRICIA: Well that union agreement is a federal one.

MARGARET: Got it.

PATRICIA: So, in a nutshell, Ansett's dragging Fly Girl to High Court next, to argue that all the wins she's had at state level shouldn't count coz this is a federal issue.

MARGARET: They've never said that before. Have they?

PATRICIA: Nah, that's some new bullshit pulled out of their legal team's arseholes. Reg and his cronies think the law doesn't apply to them. And once you learn a little bit about the law, Margie, you realise there's a million ways a rich white man can get out of obeying it.

REG IS GOD. TARMAC. JULY 15TH-ISH. 1979.

A worried-looking DEB *stands alone on the tarmac looking out to middle distance. A horrible thought enters her mind and she puts her hands to her head to stop it.*

A fairly pregnant TRISH *puffs in.*

TRISH: Sorry, my midwife appointment went over.

TRISH *gets into the cockpit of the plane. It's almost comical.*

DEB: They did not design this with you in mind. You're getting pretty big, aren't you?

TRISH: So are you. D'ya see the front of the paper this morning?

TRISH *starts doing the pre checks.*

DEB: I'm avoiding the news nowadays. I'm so sick of myself. I think Pete's sick of me too. All the attention's pissing him off.

TRISH: That's coz no-one's talking to him any more.

Beat. TRISH *stops pre-checks.*

How you holding up?

The sound of a chopper getting closer builds throughout the rest of the scene.

DEB: I dunno. Worried about money, I guess. Even with people donating it's— … and Pete and I have been fighting … a lot.

TRISH: You've had a pretty stressful start to your marriage.

DEB: I keep having this dream that all these men, dressed in orange, are trying to break into the house. Banging down doors, smashing through windows, coming down the chimney. I mean, we don't even have a chimney. And I wake up thinking this whole thing's been one big nightmare. But it's actually happening.

Beat.

When I said I'd fight this to the end … it never occurred to me there might not be one.

Beat.

An announcement comes over the radio in the aircraft. It's the voice of a PILOT.

PILOT: Attention, Moorabbin. Alpha November Delta is transiting the Moorabbin control zone / at one thousand five hundred feet.

DEB: You're shitting / me?

TRISH: What am I missing?

DEB: That's Reg's / helicopter.

TRISH: He really choppers to work?

The sound of the chopper gets louder and DEB *raises her voice to speak over it.*

DEB: Yep.

TRISH: I thought that was an urban myth.

DEB: Nup.

TRISH: That must cost a packet.

DEB: He's got the money to do whatever the hell he wants.

DEB *looks up as the chopper gets louder.*

Someone once told me Reg was God. I thought they were joking but it's actually true. He's up there; unreachable, all powerful, controlling my whole fucking life.

REG*'s chopper flies right over the top of them.*

COCKTAILS ON THE HELIPAD. REG'S HOUSE. 1979.

The sound of REG*'s chopper continues to grow as lights up on* REG*'s* WIFE, *dressed in an evening gown, carrying a tray with a glass of whiskey atop. As the helicopter approaches, the sound grows, her hair is blown and she struggles to stand upright.* FRANK *stands off to the side, waiting as* REG *strides on.*

REG'S WIFE: Welcome home, darling.

Paying her no heed, REG *grabs the whiskey off the tray and heads towards* FRANK, *who is holding various papers that he then passes to* REG.

FRANK: Business Affairs is worried, Reg. We've held off training so long—to keep Wardley out—we're short on pilots. This week we've had to cancel flights.

Beat.

And the general feeling out there, with the press and the public is … maybe it's getting bit vengeful … maybe it's gone on long enough.

REG: Are you suggesting I give up, Frank?

FRANK: No, no, course not. It's just … Growth this quarter's three-point-four percent compared to sixteen-point-eight at TAA.

REG: This isn't about numbers Frank, it's about principles. The girl doesn't belong. Eventually she'll see that and surrender.

FRANK: I don't think she's the surrendering type.

REG *hands* FRANK *the Federal Pilots Agreement.*

What's this?

REG: Federal Pilots Agreement. Read the highlighted passage, Frank.

FRANK: ' … *The Employer has the right to terminate employment for any reason within the first twelve months.*'

REG: So, even if she wins at High Court, under *this agreement,* legally we can hire her one day, fire her the next. Mark my words, Frank, as long as I'm at Ansett, this woman will *never* pilot one of my planes.

SPREADING THE WORD 3. D-DAY GIRLCOTT. JULY 31ST. 1979.

PATRICIA *is on the phone to a whispering* GLENDA.

GLENDA: Can't talk right now, Pat!

PATRICIA: Why are you whispering?

GLENDA: Hayden's watching cricket, he doesn't like it when I make noise.

PATRICIA: Wake up, Glenda! You gotta stop doing everything Hayden tells you. If you want to change the world, first you have to change yourself.

GLENDA: I don't want to change. I feel sick just listening to you talk about it. This Girlcott's a bad idea. You're all gonna get into so much trouble.

PATRICIA: Glenda. You are what the feminists are calling '*brainwashed by the patriarchy*'.

GLENDA: What's the patriarchy?

ANGRY HAYDEN: [*voiceover*] Get us another longneck, Glenda!

GLENDA: [*calling out sweetly*] Coming, darling! [*Whispering*] Gotta go Pat.

PATRICIA: Alright, Glen. But once Hayden's passed out, I want you to grab the newspaper—

GLENDA: Hayden says I shouldn't read the news, it'll only / give me nightmares.

PATRICIA: I know. But I want you to take a look at the front page. Women's groups are calling today D-Day.

GLENDA: Why's that?

PATRICIA: It stands for 'Discrimination against Deborah Day'. Because it's a year to the day Fly Girl should have started her training.

GLENDA: Has it been that long?

PATRICIA: Yes, Glenda! They've dragged her through the courts for more than a year for the mere fact she wasn't born a man.

GLENDA: But she wasn't born a / man.

PATRICIA: So I want you to look at that front page, Glenda. Look at the fuss everyone makes when a woman goes after what she wants. Because that's the patriarchy.

THE STRAIN OF THE PRESS INVASION. PETE AND DEB'S HOME. MORNING. OCTOBER 28TH. 1979.

The phone rings and a pissed-off PETER *enters in a dressing gown and answers it.*

PETER: Yes? It's *Wardley*. Lawrie's my wife's maiden name. I don't have to answer your questions, it's seven in the morning … I'm hanging up.

PETER *hangs up and the phone and it rings again. He immediately picks up.*

Leave us alone!

PETER *hangs up. He leaves. The phone rings again. A stressed* DEB *enters in her dressing gown. She picks up.*

DEB: Hello? No. I really can't talk right now. My husband's getting pretty annoyed at the constant calls.

DEB *abruptly hangs up. The phone rings again. Pissed off,* DEB *picks it up, holds the hook switch down and places the phone off the hook. She turns to go and the doorbell rings.*

PETER: [*off*] Don't answer it, Deb! They've got no respect for our privacy!

The doorbell chimes again.

Deb?! Leave it!

A torn DEB *exits the stage and we hear a voice from outside.* PETER *slowly re-enters the lounge room to eavesdrop.*

JANA WENDT: Hello, Mrs Wardley. I'm Jana Wendt, freelance reporter. I know you're heading off to High Court tomorrow—

DEB: —it's very early and I look like shit, pardon the French, Jana … I haven't even got make-up on.

JANA WENDT: I know your supporters would really love to hear how you're feeling about it.

DEB: Right.

JANA WENDT: Pop back in, do what you have to and we'll wait here.

DEB: I guess that's decided then … Give me a minute.

An exasperated DEB *closes the door and rushes into the lounge room where a pissed-off* PETER *is standing.*

There's a reporter here.

PETER: Just say no.

DEB: I can't ignore my supporters, Pete. They're paying the court fees.

PETER: You don't ignore them, Deb. You do all their interviews, you go to their rallies and I don't understand why coz Dwyer told you to keep away from all that women's lib crap!

DEB: I can't just / say no—

PETER: You give them everything they want and they just want *more*.

DEB: I've gotta keep the *press* on side.

PETER: Tell yourself that, Deb, but really you just love the attention!

DEB: Fuck off, Pete. If anyone loves attention it's you! I saw you at the Aeroclub. With that girl.

Beat.

You looked right through me.

The truth hangs in the air. Beat.

PETER: You wanna fly more than you wanna be married.

Beat.

Tell me it's not true.

A CAR BACKFIRED. STREET. DAY. AUGUST 1979.

A strung-out DEB *walks on the street. Suddenly we hear the sound of a car backfiring.* DEB *thinks it's a gunshot and dives for the ground.*

Lights out.

SOMEONE WAS SHOOTING AT YOU. DEB'S HOUSE. AUGUST. 1979.

A paranoid and very highly strung DEB *and a distressed* MUM *in the middle of a very heightened argument.*

MUM: Someone was shooting at you?

DEB: A car backfired, it just sounded like a gunshot and before I knew it I / hit the ground.

MUM: Why would someone shoot / at you?!

DEB: Reg hates me! This whole mess would disappear if I was dead.

MUM: Don't say that, / Debbie!

DEB: Just listen, Mum! As I lay on the ground I realised: he's *not* going to kill me coz if he did, everyone would know it was him and once I realised that I felt so much better.

MUM: Well, I'm glad you felt better, Debbie, but the fact you think Reg Ansett won't murder you because he'll be the main suspect brings me no comfort. You don't eat, you don't sleep. Your marriage is falling apart and now you think people are shooting at you? How long do you think you can keep going like this?!

DEB: You know I can't / give up!

MUM: You're twenty-five years old and that man's taking the best years of your life.

DEB: Dwyer says they won't be able to hold out much / longer!

MUM: Really?! Because they've held out this long! You won the first hearing, they fired the Board. You won the second, they appealed. They lost the first grounds of their appeal, now they're dragging you to High Court. They stall and they stall and they stall and they have pockets deep enough to do that forever!

Beat. MUM *looks at* DEB *seriously and speaks softly.*

And what if this isn't the time, Debbie? What if after all the suffering, all the damage being done to your life, what if it turns out you're just clearing the way for some other girl, ten years from now, to reap the rewards of all that you're sacrificing?

HOSTIES. CHICKEN OR BEEF 2. THE GALLEY. OCT 30TH. 1979.

PATRICIA *and* GLENDA *do the dinner service.*

PATRICIA: [*to customer*] The chicken or the beef, sir?
GLENDA: So did Fly Girl *win* at the big fancy court?
PATRICIA: She won't know for months, Glenda.
GLENDA: Months? Eh I'm sick of this. When does the winning bit happen? [*To customer*] Warm bread roll?

MARGARET *enters.*

Was it a good turn-out?
MARGARET / PATRICIA: [*to customer*] The chicken or the beef, sir?
PATRICIA: Six judges, lawyers from every state, Ansett brought the whole army of orange-tied arseholes.
GLENDA: [*To customer.*] Bread roll?
PATRICIA: Basically it was a room full of white men in wigs.
MARGARET: And Fly Girl practically on her own.
GLENDA: Except for the hubby. [*To customer*] Bread roll?
PATRICIA: Nup, he was a no-show.
GLENDA: What?
MARGARET: [*to customer*] The chicken or the beef, sir? [*To* GLENDA] And her lady lawyer was off having the baby.
GLENDA: That's terrible timing. [*To customer*] Warm bread roll? [*To the* HOSTIES] What about the mad-professor type?

PATRICIA: Dwyer? Apparently he raced in ten minutes *late.* [*To customer*] The chicken or the beef, sir? [*To* GLENDA] But once he got his wig straight they say he won the day.

MARGARET / PATRICIA: [*to customer*] The chicken or the beef?

GLENDA: So what's she gonna do while she waits? [*To customer*] Warm bread roll?

MARGARET: She starts training in a coupla weeks, Glen.

GLENDA: You just said she won't know if she's *won* for months. So why is she training? [*To customer*] Bread roll?

PATRICIA: Ansett's been *ordered* to put her in the training school, Glenda. That doesn't mean they'll ever let her *fly*.

GLENDA: Well, that's confusing.

MARGARET: I'm out of chicken.

MARGARET *exits to grab more stock.*

PATRICIA: [*to customer*] The chicken or the beef, sir?

GLENDA: I'm saddened to hear about her and the husband. But I can't say I'm entirely surprised, they were always gonna have bad luck.

PATRICIA: Why's that?

GLENDA: They never had a honeymoon. [*To customer*] Warm bread roll?

HAPPY NEW YEAR. DEB AND MUM AT HOME. NEW YEAR'S EVE. 1979.

MUM *reads the newspaper to* DEB.

MUM: '*Mrs Wardley is being vindictively assailed ... in a quite inhumane and unforgivable manner through the most important course of her life.*' They got that right. The union's saying what you've been through is ' *... the most blatant and calculated attack ... in the history of the federation.*' And did you see—

MUM *picks up a different paper.*

—you made it into *The Events of Seventy-Nine*? They say you showed '*sheer persistence and courage in the face of discrimination.*' Honestly, I don't know where you get it from.

DEB: I do.

MUM: … Yes, well.

Beat.

I'm sorry your father hasn't been here through all this, Debbie.

DEB: I'm not talking about him.

Beat.

You're the one who raised four kids single-handed when Dad left. You're the one who drove me to every flying lesson when you didn't understand why I wanted to fly. And you're the one still supporting me through this endless court case even though you think I should have quit long ago. If I have persistence and courage, Mum, I got it from you.

MUM, *not used to praise, looks at* DEB, *unsure how to respond. The phone rings.* MUM *answers.*

MUM: Dorothy speaking. Oh, Trish. How's the baby? Yes she's here. Oh, okay …

[*To Deb*] Debbie, turn the telly on. On now! Quick!

MUM *hangs up the phone as* DEB *turns the TV on.* PAMELA *is on the screen.*

PAMELA: Rupert Murdoch's company increased its stake in Ansett to forty-seven percent at a cost of ninety million dollars. Ansett Transport has said Mr Murdoch would become its new CEO but Sir Reginald would remain chairman.

DEB *turns the TV off, her mind whirring.*

MUM: So, Reg isn't in charge anymore?

DEB: It doesn't look like it.

MUM: But if Reg stays on as Chairman, can he still stop you flying?

DEB *heads out of the room. A woman on a mission.*

DEB: [*over her shoulder*] I imagine that's his plan.

MUM: [*shouting off*] Where are you going?

DEB: [*off*] To find a number.

MUM: [*shouting off*] Whose number?

DEB *returns, leafing through an address book.*

DEB: Remember, a coupla years back, I taught that lovely guy John Calvert-Jones to fly?

MUM: Not ringing / any bells.

DEB: You remember, I took his mother-in-law, Elizabeth, on a flight to Deniliquin. He kept calling her 'The Dame'—which I thought was weird. Then at some point Elizabeth says, 'You know, Rupert should really think about diversifying' and I'm thinking, who calls their kid Rupert? Here it is!

DEB *finds the number, picks up the phone and starts dialling.*

Then the penny drops. I'm sitting next to Dame Elizabeth Murdoch. John Calvert-Jones is Rupert's Murdoch's brother-in-law.

DEB *finishes dialling.*

MUM: Debbie, you're not calling him on New Year's Eve.

DEB: What have I got to lose?

Beat.

Hello John, it's Deb Lawrie. Yeah, good, good … well, except I finished ground school weeks ago and I still haven't stepped foot on an aircraft. That's why I'm calling actually; I just saw your brother-in-law's taken over at Ansett and … I mean I don't even know how close you are— … Oh, Rupert's there …

DEB *covers the receiver and mouths 'He's there'.*

All I wanna do is fly, John. It's all I've ever wanted and I'd be so grateful if you'd put in a good word for me. And please pass on; if he gives me this opportunity, I will not waste it. Happy New Year to you, too.

DEB *hangs up the phone, heart racing. She looks at her* MUM *and allows herself to hope.*

PAMELA REPORTS 7. THE WIN! 1980.

A beaming PAMELA *reports.*

PAMELA: It's shaping up to be a happy new year for Deborah Wardley. In a move which will no doubt help swing public opinion back to the ailing airline, newly appointed CEO of Ansett, Rupert Murdoch, issued a memo this morning directing Ansett management to treat Mrs Wardley '*the same*' as they treat their '*male*' pilot candidates.

So, finally, after eighteen months of struggle and sacrifice, Deborah Wardley has won the battle to become Australia's first female commercial airline pilot.

ALL US GIRLS ARE BEHIND YOU. CABIN ON A PLANE. 1980

HOSTESS ANNOUNCEMENT: [*voiceover*] Welcome aboard Flight Two-Two-Five to Alice Springs. Please stow your luggage in the overhead compartments. Smaller items can be placed under the seat in front of you. Please take your seats as quickly as possible and we will get on our way. Thank you.

GLENDA, *dressed in tropical attire, carrying hand luggage, minces into the cabin in search of her seat. She stows her luggage. After a beat* HELEN, MARGARET, PATRICIA *similarly attired, enter.*

GLENDA: Girls!
MARGARET: Glenda.
HELEN: You're here!

The women head towards GLENDA. *They don't notice a quietly confident* DEB, *dressed in an ill-fitting pilot uniform, bag in hand, enter after them and sit down.*

PATRICIA: Thought Hayden might have stopped you coming.
GLENDA: Hayden can't stop me doing anything any more. I left him.
HELEN: Oh my goodness!
MARGARET: Crikey Moses!
PATRICIA: What happened?!
GLENDA: I got sick and tired of him telling me what to do.
HELEN: Good on you, Glen.

Beat.

GLENDA: Plus, I caught him in the back of the Holden rooting my cousin Delvene.
PATRICIA: That'll do it.

The HOSTIES *settle into their seats.* MARGARET *suddenly realises she's sitting directly behind* DEB. *A dumb show ensues; mouthing, pointing, peering over seats and into the aisle.*

MARGARET: Deborah Wardley?!

DEB *turns to see the* HOSTIES *excitedly staring at her.*

It is you!

MARGARET *hops out of her seat into the aisle. The other* HOSTIES *follow.*

Margaret O'Reilly, we're hosties with Ansett, well not today, / but …

HELEN: Helen. Ex-hostie, proud Girlcott member—

MARGARET: We're such big fans!

GLENDA: Glenda.

GLENDA *gives a little wave.*

PATRICIA: Pat.

PATRICIA *puts her hand out to shake* DEB*'s hand.*

You're an inspiration!

DEB *is chuffed but a little awkward.*

GLENDA: It's so funny. I was only watching you on the telly the other day.

MARGARET: Aren't they finally letting you fly?

DEB: First flight's tomorrow.

PATRICIA: And all it took was Rupert bloody Murdoch telling management to treat you like / they treat the boys.

MARGARET: They treat the boys!

HELEN: How revolutionary!

GLENDA: He seems like one of the good guys.

DEB *smiles. Beat.*

Is this your uniform?

DEB: Ah. Yep.

GLENDA: Not the best fit / is it?

HELEN: Glen!

DEB: No, she's right. But they did say, '*If you want to act like a man, dress like one.*' So, at least in that instance they were true to their word.

MARGARET: Just gotta be taken in a bit, / doesn't it?

HELEN: A pinch at the waist and a lift at the crotch / is all.

MARGARET: No reason for you to stop being a woman just because you're working with a bunch of men.

DEB *smiles—it's nice to be understood.*

DEB: Where you off to?

HELEN: Alice / Springs!

GLENDA: Hen's / weekend.

PATRICIA: In honour of Margie.

DEB: When's the wedding?

MARGARET: Six weeks.

GLENDA: [*sadly*] Then there'll only be two of us left.

DEB: You can't be a married Hostess, can you?

MARGARET: They won't allow it.

PATRICIA: But maybe that'll change with Reg on the way out.

An announcement rings out over the PA.

FIRST OFFICER WOODBRIDGE: [*voiceover*] Welcome aboard. Please take your seats and fasten your seat belts.

GLENDA *and* HELEN *squeal and jump up and down.*

GLENDA: We're off / girls!

HELEN: Better / sit down.

PATRICIA: Don't want to be *those* passengers.

DEB: Have a nice flight.

GLENDA: Thanks, Deb. We'll try to give you some peace.

HELEN: All the best, Deb. What a treat.

PATRICIA: It was an honour to meet you.

The HOSTIES *fasten their seatbelts. Beat.* MARGARET *who is sitting directly behind* DEB *pokes her head around and taps* DEB *on the shoulder.*

MARGARET: Deborah. I just wanted to thank you for all that you've done for us.

DEB: Can I be honest?

MARGARET *nods.*

I never set out to do this for anyone but me. If other people benefit from my fight, I'm glad, but it's not why I did it. All I was fighting for was the right to spend my life doing what I love.

MARGARET: Well … now we all know that's an option.

Beat.

Anyway, such a joy to meet you. I'll leave you alone now.

DEB: Fingers crossed I'll see you on the flight deck before you leave.

MARGARET: Wouldn't that be something.

MARGARET *disappears behind* DEB*'s seat. Beat.* MARGARET *pokes her head around and taps* DEB *on the shoulder.*

MARGARET: And Deborah—

DEB *turns back to* MARGARET.

All us girls are behind you.

MARGARET *disappears behind* DEB*'s seat.*

Sound and lighting shift. DEB *is alone.*

The ACTORS *one by one stand at their seats, break the fourth wall and tell the audience the following information.*

Maybe—after each passage—the HOSTIES *leave, taking a piece of* DEB*'s uniform* [*hat, etc.*], *with the last person helping her into the coat she wore as a little girl.*

ACTOR MARGARET: On January sixteenth 1980, Deborah Jane Lawrie made Australian aviation history when she became the first female to co-pilot a flight for a major domestic airline. Ansett Flight Two-Three-Two from Alice Springs to Darwin.

ACTOR HELEN: On March fourth 1980, the High Court brought down their decision in support of Deborah Lawrie and the state legislation; four judges to two. The appeal was dismissed. Ansett was ordered to pay all Lawrie's legal costs.

ACTOR GLENDA: In 2019, Deb was awarded an Order Of Australia for '*significant service to aviation and to women in the profession*'.

ACTOR PATRICIA: In 2020, she was inducted into the Aviation Hall of Fame and became the longest-serving female commercial airline pilot in the world. Deb is still flying with a commercial airline today.

ACTOR DEB: In 2023, Sydney Airport unveiled a new bridge.
They named it the DEBORAH LAWRIE FLYOVER.
It runs straight over Reg Ansett Drive.

The lights fade. Spot on DEB.

We see THE LINE at Flemington Racecourse from the beginning of the play.

DEB *slides her foot to the line.*

She slides it over the line.

Blackout.

THE END

FLY GIRL

BY GENEVIEVE HEGNEY & CATHERINE MOORE

ENSEMBLE THEATRE
DIRECTED BY JANINE WATSON
17 OCTOBER 2025 — 22 NOVEMBER 2025
WORLD PREMIERE

Ensemble Theatre proudly acknowledges the Cammeraygal people of the Eora Nation as Traditional Custodians of the land on which we stand and share our stories. We pay our respects to Elders past and present.

CAST

GENEVIEVE HEGNEY PATRICIA, PAMELA, REG, TODD, HENRY, TRISH & VARIOUS

ALEX KIRWAN PETER WARDLEY, HELEN, GARTH, BRUCE, CAPTAIN TOMLIN & VARIOUS

CLEO MEINCK DEBORAH LAWRIE (DEB)

CATHERINE MOORE GLENDA, FAY, KENNETH, FRANK, CAPTAIN BALL, MARY & VARIOUS

EMMA PALMER MUM, MARGARET, RICHARD, CAPTAIN BURNETT, DWYER & VARIOUS

CREATIVES

PLAYWRIGHTS GENEVIEVE HEGNEY & CATHERINE MOORE

DIRECTOR JANINE WATSON

SET & COSTUME DESIGNER GRACE DEACON

LIGHTING DESIGNER MORGAN MORONEY

COMPOSER & SOUND DESIGNER DANIEL HERTEN

STAGE MANAGER ZOE DAVIS

ASSISTANT STAGE MANAGER ALEXIS WORTHING

COSTUME SUPERVISOR RENATA BESLIK

RUNNING TIME 2HRS 15MINS (INCL. INTERVAL)

REC. AGES 12+

CONTAINS ADULT THEMES, OCCASIONAL COARSE LANGUAGE

This story is based on actual events. However certain details, characters, and timelines have been changed for dramatic purposes and certain characters may be composites or entirely fictitious.

This production is made possible by:

Blake Beckett Trust.

ABOUT ENSEMBLE THEATRE

Ensemble Theatre is the longest continuously running professional theatre company in Australia and is committed to collaborating with exceptional playwrights and creative talent to present the best international plays, modern classics and new Australian works.

PLAYWRIGHTS' NOTE

It was January 2023 when the Artistic Director of Ensemble Theatre, Mark Kilmurry, emailed us an article, his wife Jacqui had sent him, about an Australian pilot named Deborah Lawrie. He asked if we'd be keen to write a play based on her story believing we'd bring a sense of *"the comic (and dramatic) to this woman's great struggle."*

The article, which spoke of Deb's fight against Reg Ansett to become Australia's first female commercial airline pilot was incredibly compelling. But it was the fact Reg believed Air Hostesses were *"old boilers"* by age 28 and that women's menstrual cycles made them *"unsuitable"* to fly planes that convinced us we were the right *"old boilers"* to tell this story.

We ended up down a rabbit hole; amazed and dumbfounded not only by what Deb had been through but also that we were not aware of this incredible woman. We emailed Mark and said that if we could have genius director Janine Watson along for the ride we were up to the challenge of trying to write this; inspirational, sprawling, legal, political, personal play that would require a cast of fifty actors. He replied, *"You can have five!"*

In the late 70's, at just 25 years old, Deborah Lawrie withstood the most unbelievable pressure for more than 18 months to become the first person to win a case under the Sex Discrimination Act. Her win paved the way for all Australian working women. Deb is a trailblazer in the true sense of the word. Over the last few years, we have had the privilege of getting to know the woman behind the legend. Deb is quietly formidable, unpretentious, witty and has more humility than one would expect from someone who has had such a profound effect on the world. She has been gracious and abundantly generous in sharing her life story with us.

We would like to thank The Commissioners' Circle for whose financial support allowed us to develop this play. Mark Kilmurry for seeing the playwright within each of us before we saw it in ourselves. And for his continuing support. Director Janine Watson our North Star whose remarkable artistic talent, wholehearted commitment and deep intelligence has helped to shape this new work. And Deb Lawrie for trusting us to tell her story.

GENEVIEVE HEGNEY AND CATHERINE MOORE
PLAYWRIGHTS

DIRECTOR'S NOTE

What an immense privilege to have been a part of the development of *FLY GIRL* for the last two years, and to direct the World Premiere of this incredible new play. This is my third collaboration with Genevieve Hegney and Catherine Moore, who I just adore, and who have made my life infinitely funnier. In *FLY GIRL*, they have captured the heart and spirit of Deborah Lawrie. Deb is generous, kind, humble and honest. She's a leader, a teacher, a pioneer and an absolute game changer. I'm in awe of her. And when you see this story, you will be too.

FLY GIRL teems with life. Gen and Cath's writing fizzes and crackles on the page. So, when the actors take to the floor and perform their words, the rehearsal room practically bursts with energy. The scope of Deb's story is vast and sprawling, yet Gen and Cath have been precise, incisive and clear-sighted in their vision of it. The momentum of their writing sweeps us along. The funnies are extremely funny, the emotional power gut-wrenching. My job in directing the play has been to wrangle it without stifling it. To craft it without containing it. My love and thanks to the exceptional cast and creative team for aiding and abetting the madness.

I'm deeply grateful for this experience. I'm grateful for Deb's grit. She is a force—her fight for professional equality nearly fifty years ago created a slipstream of inclusion that still pulls us along today.

(I want to thank my dad, Mike Watson, for recording all the Air Traffic Control announcements in this production of FLY GIRL. *He was an Air Traffic Controller at Moorabbin Airport when Deb worked there in the late 1970s, and the opportunity to honour that synchronicity was too good to pass up.)*

JANINE WATSON
DIRECTOR

PLAYWRIGHTS' BIOGRAPHY

Catherine Moore and Genevieve Hegney have been acting, singing, teaching, producing, directing, devising, coaching and improvising across film, television and theatre for over 25 years.

They have been involved in numerous creative developments across Australia including Inscription's New Australian Works project under the guidance of Kristin Linklater and Edward Albee. They have also workshopped and performed in new works by Alana Valantine, Susie Miller, David Williamson and Tony McNamara.

As a writer and creator Catherine self-devised and performed in A JAQUES BREL CABARET and WEILL WOMEN which won Pick of the Fringe at the Melbourne Fringe Festival and earned a Green Room nomination.

Genevieve co-wrote, co-produced and acted in short film THE AMBER AMULET which won numerous awards worldwide, including THE CRYSTAL BEAR at Berlin International Film Festival and an AWGIE for Best Screenplay in a Short Film.

In 2018, Genevieve and Catherine were encouraged by Artistic Director Mark Kilmurry to co-write and co-star in their first play UNQUALIFIED for the Ensemble Theatre. This two-woman show enjoyed a sold-out season and they were commissioned to write the 2022 sequel, STILL UNQUALIFIED. They subsequently received funding from Screen West and Screen Australia to adapt UNQUALIFIED for the screen.

Genevieve and Catherine's third play and latest collaboration, FLY GIRL, was commissioned by Mark Kilmurry at Ensemble Theatre and supported by The Commissioners' Circle. FLY GIRL won the Blake Beckett Trust Female Playwrights Award in 2025. Their next collaboration will be an adaption of FLY GIRL for the screen.

GENEVIEVE HEGNEY

PLAYWRIGHT & CAST — PATRICIA, PAMELA, REG, TODD, HENRY, TRISH & VARIOUS

Ensemble Theatre: UNQUALIFIED (co-writer), UNQUALIFIED 2: STILL UNQUALIFIED (co-writer). Bell Shakespeare: TWELFTH NIGHT, ANTONY & CLEOPATRA, JULIUS CAESAR, MUCH ADO ABOUT NOTHING. Belvoir: PARRAMATTA GIRLS, LOVE. Sydney Theatre Company: TOT MOM, INFLUENCE. Film: RIPTIDE, THE LITTLE DEATH. Television: COLIN FROM ACCOUNTS (S1&S2), SUNNY NIGHTS, ALL HER FAULT, IN OUR BLOOD, PIECES OF HER, YOUNG ROCK, THE COMMONS, DIARY OF AN UBER DRIVER, DOCTOR DOCTOR (S2, 3), JANET KING (S2), THE KETTERING INCIDENT, THE MOODYS, CAMP, DEVIL'S DUST. Training: National Institute of Dramatic Arts, Bachelor of Dramatic Arts 1999, University of Western Australia, Bachelor of Arts 1996.

CATHERINE MOORE

PLAYWRIGHT & CAST — GLENDA, FAY, KENNETH, FRANK, CAPTAIN BALL, MARY & VARIOUS

Ensemble Theatre: UNQUALIFIED 2: STILL UNQUALIFIED (co-writer), UNQUALIFIED (co-writer), BECKY SHAW, CASANOVA, AND THE COW JUMPED OVER THE MOON, YOU TALKIN' TO ME? THE DIARY OF AN OLYMPIC CABBIE. Bell Shakespeare: THE COMEDY OF ERRORS, AS YOU LIKE IT. Black Swan State Theatre Company: SPEAKING IN TONGUES, THE TEMPEST, FAR AWAY. Darlinghurst Theatre Company: MEMORY OF WATER. Griffin Theatre Company: THE SEVEN NEEDS, MOTORTOWN. Film: BIRTHRIGHT, RUNT, HOW TO PLEASE A WOMAN, H IS FOR HAPPINESS, BEING GAVIN, CELESTIAL AVENUE.

Television: THE TWELVE (S3), INVISIBLE BOYS, ITCH (S1, 2), DROP DEAD WEIRD (S2), JANET KING (S3), HOME AND AWAY, THE KETTERING INCIDENT, A MOODY CHRISTMAS, CROWNIES, RAKE, SPIRITED (S1, 2), CHANDON PICTURES, BIG REEF. Training: Victorian College of the Arts School of Drama 2001.

JANINE WATSON
DIRECTOR

Directing Credits: Ensemble Theatre: ARIA, COLDER THAN HERE, ALONE IT STANDS, A BROADCAST COUP, NEARER THE GODS, STILL UNQUALIFIED, UNQUALIFIED. Bell Shakespeare: THE COMEDY OF ERRORS, ROMEO AND JULIET. Redline Productions: FIERCE, CRIMES OF THE HEART, DOLORES (co-director). Acting Credits: Ensemble Theatre: A VIEW FROM THE BRIDGE. Bell Shakespeare: KING LEAR, THE DREAM. Griffin Theatre: THE HAPPY PRINCE. Little Ones Theatre: DANGEROUS LIAISONS, DRACULA. Old Fitz: MARY JANE. Sport For Jove: THREE SISTERS. Film: THE CODE. Television: THE SECRETS SHE KEEPS, NEIGHBOURS, THAT'S NOT ME. Training: National Theatre Drama School (Melbourne). Awards: Sandra Bates Directing Award 2016. Sydney Theatre Award – Best Lead Female Performance THE HAPPY PRINCE 2019. GLUG Award – Best Supporting Actress A VIEW FROM THE BRIDGE.

ALEX KIRWAN
CAST — PETER WARDLEY, HELEN, GARTH, BRUCE, CAPTAIN TOMLIN & VARIOUS

Ensemble Theatre: FLY GIRL Debut. Bell Shakespeare Theatre: HENRY V. Black Swan State Theatre: THE SHEPHERD'S HUT Creative Development. Perth Fringe Festival: WITH FIRE IN

HER HEART. Short Film: BOY ON FIRE, THE LAST TRIP, BI BI BABY. Training: Western Australian Academy of Performing Arts, Acting Bachelor Degree and Acting Diploma.

CLEO MEINCK
CAST — DEBORAH LAWRIE (DEB)

Ensemble Theatre: FLY GIRL Debut. Short & Sweet Theatre: THE FINAL ROUND. Western Australian Academy of Performing Arts: LADY MACBETH, LOVE & INFORMATION, THE CRUCIBLE. Television: THE ARTFUL DODGER S2. Film: STUBBORNLY HERE. Awards: 2024 Enjoy Film Festival – Best Actress Award Winner for STUBBORNLY HERE, WA Screen Culture Awards – Performance Award Nomination for STUBBORNLY HERE. Training: The Western Australian Academy of Performing Arts.

EMMA PALMER
CAST — MUM, MARGARET, RICHARD, CAPTAIN BURNETT, DWYER & VARIOUS

Ensemble Theatre: THE QUEEN'S NANNY, BENEFACTORS, CRUNCH TIME, RELATIVELY SPEAKING. Critical Stages: SYNCOPATION. Darlinghurst Theatre: KINDERTRANSPORT, REMEMBERING PIRATES, CONSTELLATIONS, RIDE, FOURPLAY, THE JUNGLE. Griffin Theatre: THE KID, ON THE SHORE OF THE WIDE WORLD. Melbourne Festival: THE TROUBLE WITH HARRY. Sport for Jove: THE PLAYER KINGS, ROMEO & JULIET, ROSE RIOT. Sydney Theatre Company: TOT MOM, THE LOST ECHO. The National Theatre UK/Global Creatures: WAR HORSE. Television: PLAY SCHOOL, PIECES OF HER, ALL SAINTS, UNDERBELLY: A TALE OF TWO CITIES, OFFSIDE,

BIKIE WARS, GASP! Training: National Institute of Dramatic Art.

GRACE DEACON
SET & COSTUME DESIGNER

Ensemble Theatre: THE GLASS MENAGERIE. Belvoir Street Theatre: NEVER CLOSER, WELL-BEHAVED WOMEN, TIDDAS. 25A Belvoir: HOT TUB, THE ITALIANS, NEVER CLOSER, WHO'S AFRAID, AN OX STOOD ON MY TONGUE, DESTROY, SHE SAID. Arts Centre Melbourne: LA CAGE AUX FOLLES. Melbourne Comedy Festival: NOT TODAY, SENSER. Kings Cross Theatre: AUSTRALIAN OPEN. Theatreworks: PEAR SHAPED, SENSER, PAPER STARS. International Grammar School: MAMMA MIA THE MUSICAL. Film: FROM ALL SIDES, THE HORRIFIC MURDER OF GRIGORI RASPUTIN. Television: DANCING WITH THE STARS (BBC). GLADIATORS, THE MASKED SINGER (Warner Bros). Awards: William Fletcher Foundation Scholarship, Peter Ivany Scholarship for Excellence in Design, Sydney Theatre Awards (2023, 2024). Training: National Institute of Dramatic Art (Bachelor of Design for Performance, Masters of Design).

MORGAN MORONEY
LIGHTING DESIGNER

Ensemble Theatre: EMERALD CITY, COLDER THAN HERE, THE QUEEN'S NANNY & TOUR, SUDDENLY LAST SUMMER, CLYDE'S, MR BAILEY'S MINDER. Australian Brandenburg Orchestra: INFERNO. Australian Theatre for Young People: SAPLINGS, SHACK. Belvoir: SONG OF FIRST DESIRE, AUGUST: OSAGE COUNTY, NAYIKA: A DANCING GIRL, SHITTY (25A). Essential Workers:

COLLAPSIBLE. Hayes Theatre Company: TURN OF THE SCREW. National Theatre of Parramatta: GIRLS IN BOYS CARS, A PRACTICAL GUIDE TO SELF-DEFENCE. Opera Australia: BARBER OF SEVILLE & TOUR. Pinchgut Opera: DIDO AND AENEAS, LA SERVA PADRONA. Redline Productions: CLEANSED. Sugary Rum Productions: ANATOMY OF A SUICIDE. Video Designer: Ensemble Theatre: UNQUALIFIED, A LETTER FOR MOLLY. Sydney Chamber Opera: APHRODITE. Assistant Lighting Designer: Opera Australia: PHANTOM OF THE OPERA ON SYDNEY HARBOUR. Associate Lighting Designer: Sydney Theatre Company: DRACULA.

DANIEL HERTEN
COMPOSER & SOUND DESIGNER

Ensemble Theatre: THE HALF-LIFE OF MARIE CURIE. Belvoir Theatre: GRIEF IS THE THING WITH FEATHERS. Darlinghurst Theatre: LET THE RIGHT ONE IN. Erth Visual & Physical Inc: ARC. Essential Workers: COLLAPSIBLE. Griffin Theatre: THE LEWIS TRILOGY, WHITEFELLA YELLA TREE. Hayes Theatre: MURDER FOR TWO, RIDE THE CYCLONE, FLAT EARTHERS THE MUSICAL, THE PIRATES OF PENZANCE. National Theatre Of Parramatta: FADE. Redline Productions: THE CHAIRS, HAND TO GOD. Sydney Festival: WILLIAM YANG: MILESTONE, SET PIECE. Sydney Theatre: CIRCLE MIRROR TRANSFORMATION, RULES FOR LIVING. Michael Cassel Group: THE PICTURE OF DORIAN GRAY (BROADWAY TOUR). Awards: THE PICTURE OF DORIAN GRAY (Best Sound Design of a Play Nomination, Tony Awards), THE LEWIS TRILOGY (Best Sound Design and Composition of a Mainstage Production Nomination, Sydney Theatre Awards).

ZOE DAVIS
STAGE MANAGER

Belvoir Street Theatre: THE CURIOUS INCIDENT OF THE DOG IN THE NIGHTTIME. Force Majeure: GURR ERA OP (Development). Ground Floor Theatre Company: THREE PLAYS. Melbourne Theatre Company: SUNDAY (with Sydney Theatre Company) Sydney Theatre Company: HAPPY DAYS, 4000 MILES, INTO THE SHIMMERING WORLD, RBG: OF MANY ONE (Rehearsal), IS GOD IS (with Melbourne Theatre Company), ON THE BEACH, DON'T GO GENTLE, HUBRIS AND HUMILIATION. Training: The National Institute of Dramatic Art.

ALEXIS WORTHING
ASSISTANT STAGE MANAGER

Ensemble Theatre: THE GREAT DIVIDE, THE MEMORY OF WATER, CLYDE'S. Australian Theatre for Young People: M. ROCK. Hayes Theatre: MURDER FOR TWO, NICE WORK IF YOU CAN GET IT. Little Trojan Theatre Co: PEOPLE WILL THINK YOU DON'T LOVE ME. PYT Fairfield: THE HEN HOUSE. Siren Theatre Co: THE PAST IS A WILD PARTY. Sour Cherry Productions: PROBE. Sydney Conservatorium of Music: PARRWANG LIFTS THE SKY. The Heritage Arts Company: VAULT Festival, London. Training: The National Institute of Dramatic Art.

RENATA BESLIK
COSTUME SUPERVISOR

Ensemble Theatre: TRUE WEST, HOW TO PLOT A HIT IN TWO DAYS, EMERALD CITY, ARIA, UNCLE VANYA, MASTER CLASS, ULSTER AMERICAN, SWITZERLAND, ALONE IT STANDS, THE GREAT DIVIDE, THE MEMORY OF WATER, SUMMER OF HAROLD, MR BAILEY'S MINDER, BENEFACTORS, RHINESTONE REX AND MISS MONICA, THE CARETAKER, PHOTOGRAPH 51, THE ONE, OUTDATED, CRUNCH TIME, BABY DOLL, FOLK, LUNA GALE, and many more. Bell Shakespeare: HENRY V, THE WINTER'S TALE, MACBETH. Belvoir St Theatre: FANGIRLS. New Theatricals: DARKNESS. National Institute of Dramatic Art: THE GOVERNMENT INSPECTOR, STAY HAPPY KEEP SMILING, THE TEMPEST, WOYCECK, A LIE OF THE MIND, PORT, THE THREESOME. Pinchgut Opera: THE FAIRY QUEEN, JULIUS CAESAR, RINALDO, MÉDÉE, PLATÉE and many more. Sydney Festival: BETTY BLOKKBUSTER RE-IMAGINED. Australian Chamber Orchestra: THE NUTCRACKER.

SUPPORT US

Every dollar counts. Ensemble relies on self-earned income to deliver all the programs that we do – commissioning new work, education outreach, producing world premieres, so please think about your capacity to make a gift to Ensemble. You can donate online at ensemble.com.au/support-us or contact Stephen Attfield, Philanthropy & Partnerships Manager, on **stephena@ensemble.com.au** or via **02 8918 3400.**

LIFE PATRONS

Those who have made significant contributions to Ensemble:

The Balnaves Foundation
Clitheroe Foundation
Jinnie & Ross Gavin
Ingrid Kaiser
Graham McConnochie
Neilson Foundation
Jenny Reynolds & Guy Reynolds AO
George & Diana Shirling
Southern Steel Group Pty Ltd

PLATINUM $20,000+

The Balnaves Foundation
Giving Support Foundation
Graham Bradley AM & Charlene Bradley
Clitheroe Foundation
Ingrid Kaiser
McConnochie Family Fund
Neilson Foundation
Hon. Warwick Smith AO & Kathryn Smith
Southern Steel Group Pty Ltd
Christine Thomson
Anonymous x 1

GOLD $10,000+

Diane Balnaves
Darin Cooper Foundation
Debbie, Garry & Val
APS Foundation - Brent & Vicki Emmett Giving Fund
Alan Gunn & Kerri Fogg
Jinnie & Ross Gavin
In Memory of John Power
Jenny Reynolds & Guy Reynolds AO
George & Diana Shirling
John & Diana Smythe Foundation
Jane Tham & Philip Maxwell
Steve & Julie Murphy
Annie & Graham Williams
Anonymous x 1

SILVER $5,000+

David Z Burger Foundation
Wayne Cahill
Peter Eichhorn & Anne Willems
The Giving Fund & Sally Collier
Prue & Andrew Kennard
Helen Markiewicz
Alan & Pauline Plumb
Simon Poole AO & Louise Cardenas-Poole
David Pumphrey OAM & Jill Pumphrey
Anonymous x 1

BRONZE $1,000+

Melanie & Michael America
Margaret Andrews
Paul Bedbrook & Fiona Hopkins
Ellen Borda
Anne Bruning
Viktoriya Butler & Steven Reynolds
Alison Carmine
Margaret Cassidy
David & Caroline Champion
Anne Clark
Friends of Tracey Trinder
Debby Cramer
Valerie Crawford
Ralph Davis
Laurence Dillon
Nancy Fox AM & Bruce Arnold
Bruce & Jo Hambrett
Richard Hansford
Matilda Hartwell
Yvonne Hazell OAM
Jacqueline Katz
John Lewis
Peter Lowry AM & Dr Carolyn Lowry OAM
Catriona Morgan-Hunn
Peter EJ Murray
Barbara Osborne
Jim & Maggie Pritchitt
Dorelle & Bruce Propert
Angus & Elspeth Richards
Monica & Gary Robinson
Megan & Tim Sjoquist
Holly Stein
Bob Taffel
Neil Tait
Geoffrey Tebbutt
Judy Thomson
Lynn Trainor
Wendy Trevor Jones
Gai & Tony Wales
Dr Eric Wegman
Janice Wilkinson
Julia Wokes
Anonymous x 8

COMMISSIONERS' CIRCLE

Supporting new Australian work

Diane Balnaves
Graham Bradley AM & Charlene Bradley
Paul Clitheroe AM & Vicki Clitheroe
Jennifer Darin & Dennis Cooper
Alan Gunn & Kerri Fogg
Ingrid Kaiser
Steve & Julie Murphy
Alicia Powell
Jenny Reynolds & Guy Reynolds AO
George & Diana Shirling
Jane Tham & Philip Maxwell
Christine Thomson

LEAVE A LEGACY

We would like to thank the following Estates for their generous donations

Estate of the late Freddie Bluhm
Estate of the late Jayati Dutta
Estate of the late Jennifer Fulton
Estate of the late Helen Gordon
Estate of the late Leo Mamontoff
Estates of the late Zika & Dimitry Nesteroff
Estate of the late Margaret Stenhouse

ENCORE CIRCLE

Thank you to the following people for bequests in their wills:

Liz Barton
Valerie Crawford
Mark Midwinter
Joe Sbarro
Junia Vaz de Melo
Anonymous x 6

Supporters are recognised for 12 months from the date of donation. Current at 4 September 2025.

OUR PARTNERS

Thank you to our partners for playing a vital role in our success.

MAJOR PARTNER

ASSOCIATE PARTNER

STRATEGIC PARTNER

SUPPORTING PARTNERS

ENSEMBLE ED PARTNERS

ENSEMBLE HOSPITALITY PARTNERS

ENSEMBLE THEATRE TEAM

Artistic Director **Mark Kilmurry**
Executive Director **Loretta Busby**
Chief Financial Officer **David Balfour Wright**
Senior Producer **Carly Pickard**
Associate Producer **Saint Clair**
Literary Manager **Sarah Odillo Maher**
Production Manager **Paisley Williams**
Technical Manager **Gayda de Mesa**
Resident Stage Manager **Lauren Tulloh**
Philanthropy and Partnerships Manager **Stephen Attfield**
Marketing Manager **Rachael McDonnell**
Deputy Marketing Manager **Charlotte Burgess**
Education and Community Coordinator **Sophie Kelly**
Marketing Assistant **Emma Garden**
Media Relations **Kabuku PR**
Administrative Support **Jordan Gillett**
In-house Designer **Cheryl Ward**
Ticketing Services Manager **Spiros Hristias**
Ticketing Customer Service and Office Coordinator **Aimee Timmins**
Box Office Team **Mary Barakate, Kyra Belford-Thomas, Allan Lyra Chang, Joe Eccleston, Angus Evans, Alishia Keane, Marina McCaul & Kathryn Siely**
Finance Assistant **Gita Sugiyanto**
Front of House Manager **Jim Birch**
Front of House Supervisors **Megan Cribb, Jaro Murany, Ben Sullivan & Bella Wellstead**
Head Chef **Ian Paul Aguilar Alarcon**
Restaurant Manager **Amy Mitchell**
Building Manager **Paul Craig**

ENSEMBLE LIMITED BOARD

Chair Graham Bradley AM, John Bayley, Narelle Beattie, Mark Kilmurry, Anne-Marie McGinty, James Sherrard & Trent Zimmerman

ENSEMBLE FOUNDATION BOARD

Chair Paul Clitheroe AM, Diane Balnaves, Graham Bradley AM, Alison Cameron, Joanne Cunningham, Ross Gavin, Mark Kilmurry & David Pumphrey OAM

ENSEMBLE AMBASSADORS

Todd McKenney, Brian Meegan, Georgie Parker & Kate Raison